FISH
AND SHELLFISH

By George Lassalle
Illustrated by Alan Cracknell

SAINSBURY · WALKER BOOKS

To two favourite hostesses,
Margaret Hoffenberg and Pru Seymour

SAINSBURY CLASSIC COOKBOOKS
Series editor: Jill Norman
Designer: Jim Bunker

Published exclusively for
J Sainsbury plc
Stamford Street London SE1 9LL
by Walker Books Ltd
184-192 Drummond Street
London NW1 3HP

First published 1986

ISBN 0-7445-0657-3

CONTENTS

INTRODUCTION

For over three years now I have been haunted by a short newspaper report to the effect that a whole generation of cooks under the age of thirty was largely unfamiliar with fresh fish. I drew little comfort from a BBC World Service programme: a regular feature dealing with the Merchant Navy, paradoxically implying that we no longer have one, that our fishing industry hardly exists, and that we no longer have two ocean-going trawlers to rub together. Then, suddenly last summer, when I began to consider the writing of this book, *Fish and Shellfish*, I received a fascinating newsletter from which I feel impelled, with the author's kind permission, to quote the following paragraphs.

'Island race we may be but we eat very little fish. 5 oz per person per week is the (terribly low) figure fish authorities arrive at; and if only fresh fish, not frozen, is considered, our average consumption dwindles much more alarmingly to 1 lb *per household* every 5 weeks. How has this happened and what can we do about it? The more one thinks about it the more lunatic it seems that the harvest of the seas with which we are surrounded, a food which is so rich in nutritional value, containing a high percentage of protein and a high proportion of *unsaturated* fat, is relatively speaking so greatly undervalued . . .

'If none of us does anything one sees a situation in just a few years' time in which fresh fish is virtually unobtainable and our children, though familiar with crab sticks, find it almost inconceivable that one could eat a crab.' (David Mellor, *Cook's Commentary*, no. 3, summer 1985.)

Embedded in all statistics, others are concealed and, from the lamentable figures quoted above, the fact emerges that, for several years, vast numbers of the population have eaten no fish at all. A sad predicament for young families deprived of a source of delicious nourishment. Grim tidings for a fish fanatic such as myself, whose desire has, for decades, been to assist in promoting a healthy fish-eating and home fish-cooking habit in the nation.

How has this melancholy situation come about? Most authorities blame it chiefly on a rapid decline in 'retail outlets', that valuable and seriously threatened species, the neighbourhood wet-and-dry fishmonger, who seems, at first sight unaccountably, to have lost the support of an increasingly junk-food-consuming and carnivorous public. But the fishmonger's eventual fate might long ago have been foreseen, when the first hamburger franchise came to Britain, and that fate was sealed when a recent pope (successor of St Peter the fisherman!) dealt him a mortal blow by abolishing the willingly accepted, health-giving and economically sensible Roman Catholic discipline of fish on Friday.

In this doom-laden atmosphere, to sit down and compose a new fish cookery book seemed to call for blind faith and an almost missionary zeal. Although the simple one-line message such a book should carry was immediately clear to me – 'Fish is good for you, and fun to cook' – I reflected that the written word seemed to have lost its power to reach those most in need of instruction. Never before has there been so much space devoted to fine cookery writing. In the national press, the glossies, the important weeklies, splendid recipes of all kinds appear, and fish gets perhaps more than its fair share of coverage. But it would seem that the bulk of this splendid preachment is to the converted. I applaud the cult for fish that has been created by all this expert writing, particularly among young, sophisticated enthusiasts consuming their sashimi, gravlax and ceviche. Happily, Sainsbury's have recognised the need to encourage people to buy more fish. Look at the lavish displays of the beautiful creatures in the larger stores; there is an abundance to choose from. More fish is sold in controlled atmosphere packaging too, which keeps it fresh for a longer time. I hope that this new wealth of fish and the ideas in this book will persuade more people to try it.

George Lassalle

THE VARIETY OF FISH

For the home cook, quite apart from its manifest nutritional advantages, fish has the additional attraction, with its great variety of species, textures and flavours, of offering a vastly wide choice which cannot be matched by even the most competitive butcher, however talented and creative he is with his sharp sculpting knives, his string and his larding needle. Fish moreover is beautiful. Words can do little to convey the beauty of these triumphs of aquanautical design, and the writer must content himself with ritually intoning the litany of their noble names.

Here, however, the artist can step in to do justice to the scene: the brilliant impression of a wet-and-dry fishmonger surrounded by his tempting wares is a tribute to his stock which would nowadays include most of the fish which at one time were only seasonably available, such as salmon and trout, and certain shellfish and crustacea. Thanks to Scottish enterprise the oyster too, I hear with joy, may soon be in all-the-year-round supply. Many other fish which it would have surprised the citizen of twenty-five years ago to find at his fishmonger's, are now available. Some have been demanded by British tourists, back from Mediterranean holidays, some by fish-loving immigrants.

Now we come to the naming of names with which we should become intimately familiar:

Anchovy, angel fish, bass, bloater, bonito, bream, brill, carp, cod, coley, conger, dabs, dogfish, eel, garfish, gurnard, haddock, hake, halibut, herring, John Dory, ling, mackerel, monkfish, mullet (grey and red), pilchard, plaice, pollock, salmon, salmon trout, sardine, shad, skate, sole (Dover and lemon), sprats, tope, trout (river), tuna, turbot and whiting.

The list covers practically all fish – with the exception, for the moment, of shellfish and cephalopods – with which we are likely to have to deal. For the fish cook's convenience (not, I hasten to add, the zoologist's), they can be divided into four separate types, as the table opposite shows.

NON-OILY FISH

FIRM	SOFT
Angel fish	Cod
Bass	Coley
Bream	Dabs
Brill	Haddock
Carp	Ling
Conger	Plaice
Dogfish	Pollock
Garfish	Sole (lemon)
Hake	Whiting
Halibut	
John Dory	
Monkfish	
Mullet (grey and red)	
Skate	
Sole (Dover)	
Tope	
Turbot	

OIL-RICH FISH

FIRM	SOFT
Bonito	Anchovy
Eel	Bloater
Gurnard	Herring
Mackerel	Pilchard
Salmon	Sardine
Salmon Trout	Sprats
Shad	
Trout (river)	
Tuna	

We shall therefore approach fish in terms of these four types: non-oily and firm; oil-rich and firm; non-oily and soft; oil-rich and soft.

Note: the word 'oily' has dreadful echoes of the garage, the motorway, the juggernauts. 'Oil-rich', too, has unwelcome overtones, suggesting fishy Texans or secret hoards of cholesterol, which is the opposite of the case. In a former book, as if the fish might overhear me and be offended, I shirked the use of the word 'soft', using the term 'less firm' to describe fish which, owing to the delicacy of their texture, are quicker-cooking and more easily ruined by over-cooking than are firm fish. However we should not look on the terms 'oily' or 'soft' as being in any way derogatory.

The differing characteristics of the fish naturally influence the choice of cooking method; the time taken to cook the fish; the sauces suitable for dressing them; and the amount of fish to provide per portion. Most smoked fish are of the oil-rich type, haddock being a miraculous and happy exception. (Cod, another non-oily fish, does not smoke nearly so successfully.)

Choice of cooking method

For all oil-rich fish, grilling is the method *par excellence.* The large poached salmon, served with an oil-rich mayonnaise or a butter-opulent hollandaise, however delicious, is an absurdity in modern dietetic terms. For non-oily fish, no restriction can be put on the method of cooking. It is good grilled, perhaps better poached, and excellent cooked à la meunière. Oil-rich fish, on the other hand, are not used in soups or the making of fish stocks.

Cooking times

All fish cooks quickly, soft fish cooks very quickly. Indeed small quantities, poached in a stock, may very well be found to be cooked when the stock comes to simmering point.

Suitable dressings

Herb relishes, ketchups, vinaigrette and sauces based on purées of vegetables seem to be indicated for oil-rich fish, while for non-oily fish, all the butter-, egg-, and cream-based sauces of the great French cooking tradition can be called upon.

Size of portions

Although some professional chefs recommend that a whole fish weighing from 5 oz/150 g to 7 oz/200 g should suffice for one person, to me this suggests the shrewd administrator rather than the bonhomous cook, for it would take fine surgery indeed, at the table, to extract more than half the weight from the whole fish.

My own view is that the minimum weight of whole fish for one person should be something over 8 oz/250 g, to provide 6 oz/175 g of fillet. We can then accept this quantity as a healthy average minimum portion per person, as a main dish, accompanied by sauce, vegetables, etc. For a first or second among a number of courses, the quantity may be allowed to sink as low as 2½ oz/65 g to 3 oz/75 g. But this is not the whole story.

The quality and texture of the fish often influence the norm, for oil-rich fish are more 'filling'. For example, 5 oz/150 g of salmon will be as satisfying as 7 oz/200 g of plaice or coley. These variations in the 'filling' potential of fish types have to be taken into account. The individual quirks of human metabolisms make it impossible to define precisely the meanings of the terms 'filling' and 'satisfying'.

NOTES FOR FISH COOKS

Frozen fish

My experience with frozen fish is not extensive, though I have nothing against its use. I would not presume to contradict any instructions given by the makers on their bags or packets, and my advice is to follow them to the letter. If the result displeases, then complain at once. My own limited practice is to de-freeze frozen fish completely in the refrigerator before attempting to cook it, bearing in mind that, although thawed out, it may still be very cold deep inside, and should be allowed either to reach room temperature in the kitchen or should have allowance made in its cooking time.

Of 'boil in the bag', ready sauced items, I have nothing to say except that they are a direct disincentive to home cooking.

Preparation of fish

Normally, if you buy a fish whole, the fishmonger will, at your request, scale, decapitate, clean, fillet and skin the fish so that it is ready to cook.

Cooking times

This is a subject that makes cowards of us all. Some of the greatest cookery writers have taken refuge behind the evasive phrase, such as 'cook until it is done enough' or, more succinctly 'nicely done' or, with an abrupt abdication of all responsibility, 'until the fish is cooked'. Sadly enough, when modern writers have stood their ground and come out boldly with precise poaching or grilling times for given weights or thicknesses of fish, they have on occasion been grotesquely wide of the mark.

My own, no less fallible estimates of poaching and grilling times are given under the appropriate method headings later in this book. Otherwise, timings for given weights and thicknesses of fish are included in the various recipes.

Butter and margarine

In the making of savoury or compound butters (p. 18) home cooks are naturally welcome to use their own favourite brands of substitutes for butter.

Wine

Where wine is indicated for use in stocks and sauces, this does not mean the stale remnants of bottles left over from week-old parties. Open a new bottle as if you were going to have a glass of wine yourself (and why not do so?).

On the subject of wine to be drunk with fish, I drink both red and white with equal fervour, with a bias towards red in the case of oil-rich fish such as salmon trout and tuna.

'Finely chopped'

A personal note, this. I should perhaps apologise in advance for using in my recipes those antique phrases 'finely chopped', or 'finely ground', or 'pounded into a smooth paste', which, with all the splendid mechanised aids available to the modern home cook, may appear very much out of date. Nevertheless, there must still be kitchens here and there about the country which are not so well equipped.

In fact, I confess that fine chopping and pounding and slicing are some of the many joys I find in the recreation of cookery. These are, if you like, my form of jogging and press-ups, and keep me fit. They are marvellous exercise, especially in preserving the muscles of the arms, shoulders and chest from that 'withering on the branch' effect which is so often seen as age advances. Moreover, if one's chopping

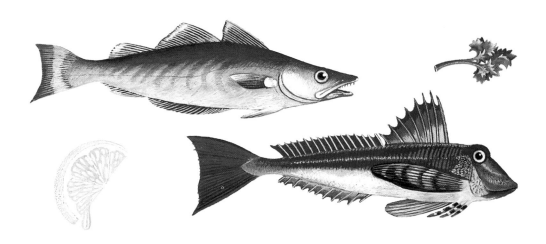

board is sited at a level enabling one to sit down to the task, then all the muscles of the lower body are also brought into play, by the practice of trotting on the spot in time with the chopping process.

KITCHEN UTENSILS

Apart from the normal equipment of household kitchens, there are few special requirements for cooking fish. Some may seem insignificant, but my own short list of the essentials is as follows.

Implements

You will need implements for lifting or turning fish without breaking them, such as broad palette knives, flat-bladed tongs, and perforated fish slices of generous breadth. For grilling over charcoal, an implement made of strong wire, which looks like two very old-fashioned tennis rackets, hinged at the top, and which grips four or five fish firmly is most welcome.

Larger items

I recommend an unusually large frying pan. I happen to possess one 20 in/50 cm by 9 in/23 cm of almost oval shape. This enables me to cook fillets or steaks of fish for six people at the same time and allows me to eat with my guests instead of staying at the stove

and cooking *en série*. It is also a splendid pan for cooking à la meunière dishes.

Fish kettles and turbotières are very expensive items, but useful if you cook fish frequently. In a small kettle you can poach a sizeable whole round fish, such as bass, bream, a whole large monkfish tail, larger sections of conger, and so on. A turbotière is useful not only for cooking the large whole flat fish, but also for poaching thick steaks and fillets of all kinds, when in some quantity.

A large chafing dish, fitted with a strainer enables cooked fish to be kept hot, without further cooking, while a sauce is completed.

A bain-marie is a wide shallow 'bath' (large pan) to contain hot water, in which finished sauces or those awaiting completion can be stood to keep hot.

Miscellanea

Some good sharp small knives; one long, very sharp knife, the tip of which can be held down on the chopping board by two fingers of one hand while the other hand moves it round in an arc as it chops herbs and vegetables; conical sieves of different sizes and gauges; a weighing machine to register very small quantities; a clock, and I almost forgot to mention

my asparagus kettle, which I have always found invaluable for making fish soups.

Crockery
Earthenware or porcelain dishes of various sizes; terrines; moulds for shaping pâtés, mousses, and so on; soufflé dishes; wide, shallow baking dishes for cooking large fish; a large platter on which to display a whole fish.

SOME USEFUL COOKING TERMS

Beurre manié
Equal quantities of butter and flour, worked together to a paste. It is added to the liquid in which food has been poached to thicken and bind it and make a sauce.

Bouquet garni
A bundle of herbs, usually thyme, parsley and bay leaf, tied with string, used for flavouring stocks and court-bouillons.

Court-bouillon
A stock composed of water, with wine or vinegar and savoury herbs and vegetables, in which fish is to be poached.

Fumet
A concentrated essence of fish and seasonings, resulting from the reduction by boiling of a strong fish stock from, say, 2 pt/1.2 litres to ½ pt/300 ml. It is used for enhancing sauces and soups. A fumet usually sets into a jelly when cold.

Marinade
A liquid usually containing vinegar, wine, herbs and spices, in which, prior to cooking, fish is laid to acquire flavour. Also a mild pickling mixture for sousing herring or mackerel.

Panada
A dough used in making fish quenelles (see p. 88).

Roux
A liaison agent in the making of sauces. It is a mixture of flour and butter in roughly equal quantities, cooked together as the basis of most sauces needing body (eg. béchamel).

METHODS OF COOKING
I give recipes for most of the fish likely to be found today, whole, or in fillets or steaks, at a good fish counter, and I have suggested sauces for each one. In every case, however, you may decide whether to make the sauce suggested or whether instead to choose and, in a matter of minutes, put together a relish or a savoury butter to accompany the dish.

1

THE DRESSING OF FISH

It is often with the approach to sauce-making that the aspirant fish cook's courage begins to fail, in contemplating the seeming vastness and illusory complexities of the subject. The ensuing pages will, I hope, completely dispel such misconceptions.

It is a critical psychological moment for the home cook. She or he has reached the point where cooking can continue to be a boring chore or it can become a happy form of mental recreation: devising and making sauces is an absorbing craft.

I recommend studying the relishes and savoury butters that follow. They are extremely simple and enable you to dress a wide range of fish at short notice.

They are followed by the five foundation sauces – the basics of French cooking.

RELISHES

CONDIMENTS, KETCHUPS AND BUTTERS

Everyone who has ever been in a fried-fish shop knows what a relish is. It is what one hopes is in those choked-up bottles on the tables. It is also what everyone has with roast lamb; namely mint sauce. It is a true relish, mint sauce, put together with mint, vinegar, water and sugar, salt, pepper perhaps. But you never find two mint sauces exactly the same. Some like it thick with mint and strong with vinegar; some like it thin in both these ingredients, with plenty of sugar; some even like it hot.

The example of mint sauce and its permutations enables me to make an important point, as I am about to propose some eighty relishes, none of which should take longer than a few minutes to make. The contents can be varied in their relative quantities as the cook desires; the quantities I give merely reflect my own taste. Each cook will discover which are to be his or her favourites. For assembling relishes, all the herbs, spices and aromatic vegetables are available to the cook. It is a limitless field.

BASIC CONSTANTS

3 fl oz/75 ml wine vinegar

3 fl oz/75 ml water

1 small anchovy fillet, finely pounded

1 small onion, finely chopped

juice of half a lemon

½ teaspoon sugar

½ teaspoon black pepper, finely ground

FLAVOURING INGREDIENTS

The flavour chosen should dominate in the relish; use in the quantities given:

1 teaspoon ground ginger
1 teaspoon creamed horseradish
1 teaspoon ground green peppercorns
1 teaspoon crushed garlic
1 teaspoon made mustard
1 teaspoon ground cumin
2 teaspoons purée of celery
2 teaspoons purée of fennel
2 teaspoons finely chopped tarragon
2 teaspoons finely chopped basil
2 teaspoons purée of capers
1 tablespoon purée of raw mushrooms
1 tablespoon purée of sweet peppers
1 tablespoon purée of gherkins
1 tablespoon purée of tomato
2 teaspoons purée of black olives

HERBS

These herbs have a special affinity with fish and one should always be present in a relish, in the quantities given:

2 teaspoons finely chopped parsley
2 teaspoons finely chopped chervil
2 teaspoons finely chopped thyme
2 teaspoons finely chopped dill
1 teaspoon ground bay leaf

Method

Select a flavouring ingredient and a herb from the lists opposite and combine them well together with the basic constants. Allow the mixture to stand for an hour before using.

These relishes are particularly effective with all oil-rich fish. They have the full status of sauces, and I am never reluctant to serve them. I only wish that they were more frequently used in restaurants.

For non-oily fish, the addition of 2 tablespoons of olive oil is an improvement, though this is not necessary. Without the olive oil, the relishes can be turned into hot butter sauces. Simply heat the relish and beat into it 2 oz/50 g butter. Keep hot, but do not let it boil.

BUTTERS: SAVOURY AND COMPOUND

As with the relishes, here again we have a plentiful supply of varied and delicious miniature sauces which can be easily made in a matter of minutes. There are at least fifty of these butters recorded in the classic canon, but this still leaves plenty of room for experiment and improvisation.

Select a herb, spice or aromatic from the flavouring ingredients opposite. The rules are few and of the simplest:

The proportion to be maintained in the butters is 4 oz/125 g butter to the same proportions of ingredients as those given in the table opposite.

In addition to your selected flavouring ingredient, there should always be included parsley, one member of the onion family (chives, shallots, spring onions, etc.), a drop or two of lemon juice, and a pinch each of salt and finely ground black pepper.

Use these butters also to make croûtons for cocktail parties and buffets. Serve them with potatoes in their jackets, and use them to season many other vegetables. They are truly all-purpose miniature sauces.

GARLIC BUTTER

This is a pattern recipe.

4 oz/125 g butter	1 teaspoon crushed garlic
2 teaspoons parsley, finely chopped	2 drops lemon juice
2 teaspoons chives, finely chopped	pinch each of salt and finely ground black pepper

Simply blend the softened butter with all the other ingredients, and put in the refrigerator to stiffen until required for use. This amount of butter will anoint sufficient fish for four or five people. It is excellent for use with all kinds of fish, especially grilled or poached fillets and steaks of non-oily fish and with fish fried à la meunière.

CREAM SAUCE

Savoury butters can also be used in making quick cream sauces.

4 oz/125 g savoury butter	1/4 pt/150 ml double cream

Put the savoury butter into a saucepan to melt on low heat. When hot, pour in the cream. Stir briskly as it comes to simmering point. Simmer for a short minute. Strain through a conical sieve, and keep warm. If you prefer a thinner sauce use single cream.

THE FOUNDATION SAUCES

These five sauces together with the relishes and butters given earlier, provide the home cook with all the tools necessary for the construction of a personal style of haute cuisine.

Béchamel and velouté are flour-based sauces the former made with milk, the latter with stock. Hollandaise and mayonnaise are mixtures of butter and oil suspended in egg yolk. Vinaigrette is a careful balance of oil, vinegar, salt and pepper, which can be embellished with herbs, mustard or shallots.

BÉCHAMEL SAUCE

Béchamel or white sauce is prolific and is the basis for many of the best sauces in the French classic repertoire. Sauces derived from béchamel and the other foundation sauces which follow will appear in the recipes.

MAKES 1 pt/600 ml SAUCE

1 1/2 oz/40 g butter	a sprig each of parsley and thyme, and a bay leaf
1 1/2 oz/40 g plain flour	
1 1/4 pt/750 ml milk, heated together with 1 small, finely chopped onion	1/4 teaspoon salt
	1/4 teaspoon ground black pepper

Melt the butter in a saucepan on low heat. Add the flour and mix well together to form a paste, and cook for about 1 minute. Remove from the stove, and add gradually the hot milk with its ingredients, stirring vigorously to effect a homogenous blending of paste and milk. Return to the stove, and keep stirring as the sauce simmers gently for 20 minutes. Remove from the heat, and allow to cool, stirring occasionally. Strain through a conical sieve.

Note: almost any savoury butter added to a béchamel, made as above, and improved with cream, produces an excellent sauce in its own right.

FISH VELOUTE

This is the basis for any number of soups and sauces for fish of all kinds; its quality and fine flavour will very much depend on the nature of the fish stock with which it is made. Here I use a good standard stock, but it must not be forgotten that every herb, spice and aromatic vegetable is available to vary its flavour, strength and style, and so radically affect the end result. No trimmings of oil-rich fish should ever be used in contriving the stock for a velouté.

MAKES 1 pt/600 ml SAUCE

For the fish stock

6 oz/175 g non-oily white fish trimmings (eg. from plaice, sole or whiting)

1 small grated carrot

½ stick celery, roughly chopped

2 shallots, roughly chopped

2 or 3 parsley sprigs

1 bay leaf

½ teaspoon salt

½ teaspoon ground black pepper

For the sauce

1½ oz/40 g butter

1½ oz/40 g plain flour

1¼ pt/750 ml fish stock

Boil the fish trimmings and all the other ingredients for the stock in 1½ pt/900 ml water for 30 minutes. Allow to cool, then strain. Proceed as for béchamel sauce (p. 19), but use the fish stock in place of the seasoned milk.

HOLLANDAISE SAUCE

Egg yolks whisked with butter over low heat thicken to form an emulsion. Hollandaise is an excellent sauce in its own right and the basis for a range of egg-thickened sauces.

MAKES 8 fl oz/250 ml

4 tablespoons wine vinegar or 2 of vinegar and 2 of lemon juice

12 peppercorns

2 egg yolks

6 oz/175 g softened, unsalted butter

½ teaspoon salt

Divide the butter into small nuts. Reduce the vinegar by boiling with the peppercorns to about 2 or 3 tablespoons of liquid and strain into another pan. Allow to cool a little. Then beat in the egg yolks with a whisk.

Now on a very low heat, or in a bain-marie (p. 14) gradually beat in half the nuts of butter and the salt. When the mixture begins to thicken, add the remaining butter, one nut at a time, whisking throughout until the mixture has the texture of thick double cream.

VARIATION

Any of the relishes on p. 16 may be reduced over heat to a few strained tablespoons of savoury liquid and be used in place of the vinegar to produce variants of hollandaise, an infinitely variable sauce for all fish, hot or cold.

MAYONNAISE

MAKES ¾ pt/450 ml

1 teaspoon powdered or made mustard	*½ teaspoon black pepper, finely ground*
2 teaspoons wine vinegar	*2 egg yolks*
1 teaspoon salt	*¾ pt/450 ml olive oil*

If using eggs taken from the refrigerator, allow the yolks time to reach room temperature. In a bowl, blend together the first five ingredients and stir for one minute. Then, drop by drop to begin with, add the olive oil. As the mixture begins to thicken pour in the oil in a thin steady stream.

VARIATIONS

Here again, the relishes (p. 16) come in handy. Reduce the relish, by boiling, to a few tablespoons. Pour through a sieve and allow to cool.

Use one teaspoon of the concentrate in lieu of the mustard, vinegar, salt and pepper in the above recipe, to blend into the egg yolks before adding the oil. You can thus make many subtle variants of mayonnaise.

VINAIGRETTE SAUCE

This in all its simplicity is the true basic vinaigrette, which makes a delicious dressing for all green and other salads, and is not to be despised as an accompaniment to grilled, fried or poached fish. In a vinaigrette, the proportion of oil to vinegar, as shown here, is three of oil to one of vinegar.

MAKES 4 fl oz/125 ml

2 tablespoons wine vinegar	*6 tablespoons olive oil*
salt and pepper	

Whisk together the vinegar, salt and pepper until thoroughly mixed. Add the oil in a steady stream, whisking as you do so. Taste for seasoning.

VARIATIONS

Any number of vinaigrettes can be made from the relishes (p. 16) by reducing the amount of vinegar in the relish recipe to 2 tablespoons and stirring into it 6 tablespoons of olive oil. Eliminate the sugar from the relish too, if you wish.

21

2
GRILLING

This is probably the first method of cooking fish adopted by *homo sapiens*, when he gave up eating it raw. Grilling is a simple process, and the skills involved are quickly learned, but preparing and controlling a charcoal grill is a skill on its own. For cooking meat, there is nothing better, but for fish, it can present problems. It is best not to remove scales or head if you are using a charcoal grill. For a large fish make 2 or 3 diagonal incisions in the thicker part of the flesh. For small fish use a well-oiled double grill to hold them in place while you turn them over. Close attention to timing is essential. For everyday use, electric and gas grills are best.

Small fish, or thin fillets or steaks, should be put to a fierce heat. Thicker fish should be put to a moderate heat or laid at some distance from the source of heat, which then has time to penetrate to the centre without overcooking or burning the outer flesh. Bear in mind that the rate of penetration of heat varies as the square of the thickness of your fish. Thus, if it takes 2 minutes to grill a thin piece of fish then to grill a piece twice as thick will take not twice as long, but four times as long. (I am grateful to be reminded of this basic law of physics by Alan Davidson, in his book *North Atlantic Seafood*.)

The following table is intended as a guide for grilling times of fully thawed fish of various thicknesses of steak or fillet that the cook will normally be called upon to deal with.

Thicknesses of fillets or steaks	Grilling times, turning over at half-time	
	Firm fish	Soft fish
½ in/1 cm	4 minutes	3 minutes
1 in/2.5 cm	10 minutes	8 minutes
1½ in/3.5 cm	12 minutes	10 minutes
2 in/5 cm	15 minutes	12 minutes

This table also applies to whole small unscored fish, measured at their thickest part.

As mentioned earlier (p. 12), if your fish is frozen, the instructions on the packet should be followed. The above table only applies to completely thawed out fish at kitchen temperature. For larger whole scored fish, frequent watching and testing with a probe provide the only reliable method.

Make sure the grilling bars are hot and well oiled before the fish is put on them to cook.

When grilling, give full attention to what you are doing. Small fillets and slender steaks, particularly of soft fish, such as plaice, coley or cod, can be cooked on one side, under a fierce heat, in less than a minute. You must be ready with the fish tongs or other implement to turn the fish over at the right moment. When a time is given in a recipe, test a little before that time is up, by probing, with a thin, sharp skewer or knife, near the bone. If any pink shows, or the flesh displays no tendency to spring away from the bone, then go to the full time given and test again.

Fish may be laid in a marinade for some time, prior to grilling, though this is not essential. A simple marinade in which the fish should be turned occasionally while it waits to be cooked is a mixture of olive oil, lemon juice or wine vinegar, bay leaf, a small chopped onion, salt and pepper. Other more elaborate marinades appear in the recipes which follow.

It is essential to baste the fish throughout the process of grilling. All that is needed is a little olive oil and lemon juice, salt and pepper and a basting brush (the type with which you brush egg or milk on pastry). Small whole fish weighing 5 oz/150 g to 7 oz/200 g can be dealt with as they are, without scoring or other attention than basting. Fish weighing 8 oz/250 g, or over, should be scored diagonally with a sharp knife on the side first to be put to the grill, and when turned, again scored diagonally in a reverse direction to the cuts on the other side, well basted, and again set to the heat. Judiciously carried out, this method of scoring will keep the fish intact and facilitate its removal to a serving dish when cooked. Whole fish weighing much over 1 lb/500 g should, for convenience, be cut into steaks for grilling.

GRILLED MACKEREL WITH GOOSEBERRY SAUCE

Mackerel is a firm and oil-rich fish calling for sweet and sour sauces, or relishes based on mustard, horseradish, capers, etc. The simple gooseberry sauce exactly matches the temperament of the fish.

SERVES 4

four 8 oz/250 g mackerel	1 shallot, finely chopped
For the marinade	**For the sauce**
½ pt/300 ml water	1 lb/500 g unripe, green, carefully topped and tailed gooseberries
3 tablespoons wine vinegar	½ pt/300 ml water
3 tablespoons olive oil	**For basting**
juice of ½ lemon	the oil from the top of the marinade
2 crushed bay leaves	
4 crushed black peppercorns	**For garnish**
2 crushed cloves	1 tablespoon parsley, finely chopped

One hour before you intend to cook them, lay the mackerel in a shallow dish to fit them, and pour over them the marinade. The liquid may not cover them: never mind; turn them over once or twice. Meanwhile prepare the sauce by boiling the gooseberries in the water until soft and thick. Pass through a sieve or blender to get a good smooth purée. Set aside to keep hot. Remove the fish from the marinade, and score each with 3 diagonal cuts. Put them under a moderate grill, cut side up, for 7 minutes, basting frequently with the top of the marinade. Remove them from the heat; turn them over carefully; and again score them diagonally (in reverse) with 3 cuts. Put them back under the grill for another 7 minutes, continuing to baste as they cook. Lay the fish in a heated serving dish, and dress the gashes with the parsley. Serve the gooseberry sauce separately.

Suggested accompaniments: plain boiled new potatoes, small baked tomatoes.

Note: the marinade given here is a good general purpose one, which may be used for other dishes. If you decide not to use it, then baste the fish as they are grilling with a mixture of olive oil and lemon juice. Marinades are refinements and not compulsory.

to the grill. Brush them well with the basting mixture, and put under a moderate grill for 7 minutes, basting frequently.

Turn the fish over, and repeat the scoring process. Return to the grill and cook for a further 7 minutes. Baste as necessary. Remove to a hot serving dish and, using a teaspoon, fill the cuts with a little of the sauce, the bulk of which should be served separately. Serve with a purée of potatoes and a very well drained purée of spinach.

GRILLED GREY MULLET WITH BERCY SAUCE

The grey mullet is the antithesis of the mackerel, being less firm of flesh and not oil-rich. A beautiful fish, aquatically streamlined, it has no very pronounced individual flavour, which invites a rich wine sauce, or a simple one, as here.

SERVES 4

four 8 oz/250 g grey mullet	*1 tablespoon parsley, finely chopped*
For the sauce	**For basting**
2 tablespoons shallot, finely chopped	*2 tablespoons olive oil*
¼ pt/150 ml dry white wine	*juice of 1 lemon*
	1 teaspoon onion, grated
¾ pt/450 ml fish velouté (p. 20)	*a good pinch of ground black pepper*
2 oz/50 g butter	*a good pinch of salt*

Make the sauce before grilling begins. Cook the chopped shallot in the wine until the wine is reduced by half. Then stir in the velouté. Heat through and finish by stirring in the butter and the parsley. Keep warm whilst cooking the fish.

As in the recipe for mackerel (p. 24), score each mullet with 3 diagonal cuts on the side to be put first

GRILLED SWORDFISH WITH BLACK BUTTER

This comparative newcomer to the British market is a fine firm fish, discreetly oil-rich, not as filling as tuna. It is good grilled, simply brushed over with lemon juice. Overcooked it can turn to cotton-wool. With black butter, a simple sauce which should be much more widely used, it is truly a gastronomic experience.

SERVES 5-6

5-6 swordfish steaks of ½ in/1 cm thickness	*¼ pt/150 ml wine vinegar*
For basting	*juice of 1 lemon*
2 tablespoons olive oil	*1 tablespoon capers, finely chopped*
juice of ½ lemon	
For black butter	
4 oz/125 g salted butter	

Cut the fish steaks in half, so that you have semi-circular segments. Seven minutes' grilling on each side under a moderate heat, basted with the oil and lemon juice mixture, should see them well enough done. Remove them to a hot serving dish.

Now put the butter to melt on a low heat in a heavy frying pan. Watch as the butter turns from *café au lait* colour to, in rapid stages, a deeper and deeper brown, until it is just about to burn. At this critical moment, slip in, down the side of the pan, the mixture of vinegar, lemon and chopped capers. There will be a great sizzling and some smoke as the cold liquid meets the sizzling butter and you stir all round for a few seconds. Distribute the sauce, piping hot, over the hot steaks, and serve.

This is an invaluable quick sauce: only half a minute from the moment your butter has melted in the pan. It should be used with all kinds of white fish fillets and steaks, as well as oil-rich fish. Definitely a sauce to remember.

GRILLED SEA BASS WITH HOLLANDAISE SAUCE

When mature, a whole sea bass extends nearly a yard – or metre – in length. Firm steaks, 1 in/2.5 cm thick, will weigh a little over ½ lb/250 g each. So 2 lb/1 kg of this fine solid non-oily fish, which is free of small bones, should be ample for 6 people, when served with butter-rich hollandaise sauce, and a supporting garnish or two. Small bass are splendid stuffed and baked or braised in the oven. They also grill well, laid on a bed of fennel to create a fine fragrance in the kitchen.

SERVES 6

2 lb/1 kg of 1 in/2.5 cm steaks of sea bass	2 teaspoons celery, finely chopped
For basting	a good pinch of ground black pepper
2 oz/50 g melted butter	
juice of ½ lemon	a good pinch of salt
For garnish	**For the sauce**
2 tablespoons parsley, finely chopped mixed with	see p. 20

The sauce, and any other items for the dish, such as garnishes and vegetables, should be completed before grilling begins. The sauce, which should not be kept waiting too long, should be stood in a bain-marie (p. 14) and whisked from time to time as grilling proceeds.

Brush the steaks with melted butter and lemon juice, put them to a moderate grill, and cook for 9 minutes on each side, basting well every 3 minutes. Remove to a hot serving dish. Sprinkle with the garnish. Take to the table; remove the skin; dissect and distribute judiciously.

Suggested accompaniment: tomatoes and/or courgettes, stuffed with cumin-spiced rice.

MONKFISH KEBABS

This is properly a recipe for a charcoal grill and an outdoor party, but it can just as easily be cooked on a normal household gas or electric grill.

SERVES 6

2 lb/1 kg monkfish tail, cut into pieces weighing roughly 1 oz/25 g each

For the marinade

4 cloves garlic, crushed and pounded

2 teaspoons ground root ginger

2 fillets of anchovy, pounded

½ pt/300 ml water

½ pt/300 ml white wine

3 tablespoons wine vinegar

juice of 1 lemon

a bouquet garni of sprigs of thyme, parsley, bay leaf

1 tablespoon ground black pepper

1 teaspoon sugar

¼ teaspoon cayenne pepper

For the skewers

1 large carrot, cut into ⅛ in/3 mm thick rounds

4 oz/125 g fennel bulb, very thinly sliced

1 small red pepper, deseeded, cut into 1 in/2.5 cm squares

1 small green pepper, deseeded, cut into 1 in/2.5 cm squares

12 mushrooms, halved

4 oz/125 g celeriac, very thinly sliced

Assemble the marinade first, so that its ingredients have time to blend while the kebab skewers are being prepared. The skewers should also be loaded well before cooking time, as they should remain in the marinade for at least an hour before they are grilled.

Take 6 long skewers and load each one with the ingredients in the following order: a round of carrot, as a 'stopper'; then a slice of fennel bulb, a square of pepper, a half mushroom, a slice of celeriac, a piece of monkfish. Repeat this succession a further 3 times, excluding the carrot of which a round should only be used again as a 'stopper' at the sharp end of the skewer. Lay the skewers in the marinade for an hour or more, turning them frequently so that they become thoroughly impregnated with the rich flavours. If you don't have a suitable dish in which to marinate the kebabs, you can marinate the cut ingredients and thread them onto skewers just before grilling.

Put the skewers to a moderate grill for 2 minutes. Then give each skewer a quarter turn, clockwise, and grill for a further 2 minutes. Repeat this process twice more (8 minutes in all). Baste frequently. Now raise the temperature of the grill and repeat the turning process, but this time at only 1 minute intervals. Total grilling time is 12 minutes, throughout which basting with the marinade should be continuous. Serve the skewers on a bed of plain boiled rice.

This recipe sounds complicated, but once the ingredients are to hand, the preparation time is not so very lengthy. Not for every day perhaps, but a recipe that's fun to follow as well as being quite delicious to consume, with a good strong wine.

VARIATION

Use huss or angel shark in place of monkfish.

27

3
POACHING

Poaching is cooking by total immersion in a vegetable and herb stock, or court-bouillon, which is heated to simmering point, but never allowed to boil. Small fish and fillets (4 oz/125 g to 6 oz/175 g) will be found to be almost cooked as the court-bouillon comes to simmering point. Fish weighing from 7 oz/200-225 g to 1 lb/500 g will be cooked in from 2-5 minutes, depending on whether the fish is in the soft or firm category. Thereafter, the following table is as reliable as most.

Weights of fish	Firm fish	Soft fish
1 lb/500 g	6 minutes	5 minutes
1½ lb/750 g	7 minutes	6 minutes
2¼ lb/1.125 kg	10 minutes	8 minutes
4½ lb/2 kg	14 minutes	10 minutes
6¾ lb/3 kg	18 minutes	15 minutes
9 lb/4 kg	28 minutes	20 minutes

COURT-BOUILLON

Here is a recipe for a fragrant court-bouillon, adaptable to oil-rich and non-oily fish. The amount given here should be enough to poach most round and fat fish in a small pan. For cooking very big fish in a fish kettle or turbotière more will be needed.

MAKES 4 pt/2.4 litres

4½ pt/2.6 litres water

2 carrots, roughly grated

2 sticks of celery, chopped

4 shallots, chopped

the white of 2 leeks, chopped

2 good sprigs of thyme

2 teaspoons tarragon, chopped

2 bay leaves

5 or 6 parsley sprigs

12 black peppercorns, crushed

6 tablespoons wine vinegar

For non-oily fish: eliminate the vinegar, add the juice of a lemon, ¼ pt/150 ml white wine and 1 teaspoon salt.

4
BAKING

Baking implies cooking in a more or less hot oven with little or no liquid. Most fish would dry out if exposed to the heat of the oven without some means of moistening them, and it is customary, however, to provide a source, however meagre, of liquid, butter or oil, with herbs and aromatics, with which the fish can be basted. This also contributes savour to the hot air circulating around it as it cooks.

Small oil-rich fish such as herring and mackerel need less basting than non-oily fish because they give off some moisture from their skins.

Whole baked fish look attractive and can be served from the dish in which they are cooked.

BAKED HERRINGS WITH MUSTARD BUTTER

The herring weight for weight is as nutritious as meat. It would be a crime if over-fishing were to eliminate it from the nation's diet. It is oil-rich and does not require a rich sauce. A sharp relish or mustard butter will point up its unique flavour. Grilling or baking them, whole, retains this flavour to a great degree. Cooking them open, a good deal of flavour is lost, as is the joy of slitting them down the back on one's plate, and inhaling the first savoury vapours.

SERVES 4

four 8 oz/250 g herrings

For baking

1/4 oz/5 g unsalted butter

2 oz/50 g mustard butter (p. 18)

1 lemon

With the unsalted butter, rub round the bottom and sides of a shallow baking dish. Score the herrings diagonally on one side, deeply but not down to the

bone, and lay them, cut side up in the baking dish. Rub the fish with the softened mustard butter, seeing that the gashes are filled. Put them in the oven, at gas 6/400°F/200°C, for 7 minutes. Remove from oven, turn the fish over carefully, and again score them diagonally, taking care to avoid coincidence with the cuts on the other side. Anoint the fish in the cuts, as before, with the mustard butter. Put them back in the oven for a further 5 minutes. Again remove from oven, baste exposed surfaces of the fish, and raise the oven to gas 8/450°F/230°C. Wait 1 minute for the temperature to rise. Put the fish back, this time on the topmost shelf of the oven, for 2 minutes. Serve with quarters of lemon, salt and pepper.

To accompany the fish, make a plateful of watercress or mustard-and-cress sandwiches, with thin brown bread and butter.

SEA BREAM WITH PIMENTO SAUCE

The bream family comes in all sizes and colours, from the 4 in/10 cm pickerel to the majestic dentex. Between these are the sea breams familiar to the British market. Oval in shape, they appear to suffer from slight spinal curvature due to their ponderous heads. They are splendid food, with easily avoided bones; good oval steaks can be got from the larger ones.

SERVES 5-6

1 sea bream of approximately 2 lb/1 kg	**For baking**
For the sauce	2 tablespoons olive oil
5 small red peppers	salt and ground black pepper
¾ pt/450 ml thick béchamel sauce (p. 19)	juice of 1 lemon
2 good pinches ground allspice	1 large Spanish onion, very finely sliced in rings

Blanch the peppers in boiling water for 1 minute. When cool, remove stalk, pith and seeds. Chop the peppers finely and blend into a purée with a few tablespoons of béchamel and then restore this to the rest. Add the allspice. The sauce is now ready, and should be kept hot, but not allowed to boil.

Brush the fish, inside and out, with a mixture of oil and lemon, salt and pepper. Likewise brush the inside of a wide shallow baking dish. Lay half the fine onion rings in the dish. Place the fish on them, and use the remaining onion rings to cover the top of the fish. Put the dish in the oven at gas 4/350°F/180°C for 25 minutes. Remove from oven. Slide the onion rings off the top, and again brush the fish with the basting mixture. Raise the oven to gas 7/425°F/220°C, and cook the fish for another 7-8 minutes.

I propose ratatouille (p. 39) as an accompaniment.

BAKED RED MULLET WITH A RATATOUILLE

These delicious fish, not related to the grey mullet, are now hardly to be found larger than 4 in/10 cm long in the Mediterranean, but they are sometimes to be found in larger sizes in British fish markets. They are rightly considered to be one of the finest flavoured of all the round fish. (The addition of one small red mullet to a fish stock imparts a very special, gamey flavour to the velouté sauces and soups for which the stock is used.)

SERVES 4

12 small 3 oz/75 g red
mullet or 8 of a larger
size: say, 6 oz/175 g

For the ratatouille

4 fl oz/125 ml olive oil

2 large onions, finely
sliced

3 cloves of garlic, crushed

4 small aubergines,
thickly chopped

1 large green pepper,
deseeded and roughly
chopped

1 large red pepper,
deseeded and roughly
chopped

4 peeled tomatoes

salt and pepper to taste

For baking

3 oz/75 g butter

2 shallots, finely chopped

1 small carrot, grated

1 tablespoon parsley,
finely chopped

1 tablespoon fennel
leaves, finely chopped

a scattering of ground
black pepper

a pinch of salt

In the olive oil, cook the onion and the garlic until both are soft, but do not let them take colour. Add the aubergines and the green and red peppers. Cook these together for 10 minutes. Add the tomatoes, salt and pepper. Cover the pan and allow to stew very gently on a very low heat for 1 hour.

In a shallow fireproof dish, on top of the stove, simmer the shallots and the carrot in the butter, till tender. Sprinkle with the parsley and fennel, pepper and salt, and stir round for 30 seconds. Lay the fish down on this buttery bed, and move them around for a few moments. Then turn them over so that both sides of all the fish have been anointed. Now, if the fish are small ones, put the dish into a hot oven (gas 8/450°F/230°C). After 3 minutes they should be turned, and baked for a further 3 minutes. If your fish are the larger ones, the oven should be set at gas 6/400°F/200°C, and the mullets baked for 5 minutes before turning and baking for another 5.

Serve the mullets in the baking dish, spooning the buttery mixture over the fish before you do so. Lemon juice is the only sauce required. Hand the ratatouille separately.

BAKED CARP PROVENCAL

This is a south of France treatment for freshwater fish which can, however, also be applied to any sizeable sea fish which comes your way. It is also a *minceur* dish, as it includes no butter, oil, milk or flour.

SERVES 6-8

one 2 lb/1 kg carp	*2 tablespoons finely chopped celeriac*
the white of 4 leeks, finely sliced	*2 tablespoons finely chopped fennel root*
1 carrot, grated	*1 sprig of rosemary*
1 large onion, finely sliced	*3 cloves of garlic, chopped and pounded*
2 sweet peppers, cleaned, deseeded and chopped	*½ pt/300 ml red wine*
1 aubergine, finely sliced	*1 teaspoon salt*
4 tomatoes, peeled and coarsely chopped	*1 teaspoon black pepper*

In a baking dish that will comfortably accommodate the fish, lay down a bed of all the herbs and vegetables listed above. Moisten it with half the wine and season with salt and pepper. Lay the fish on this savoury bed, and put it into the middle of a preheated oven, set at gas 4/350°F/180°C. Let it cook for 45 minutes, then test with a sharp-pointed knife, near the spine. Remove the fish to a large serving dish. Open it down the back and remove the main bone. Cover and keep hot. Now, on the top of the stove, add the rest of the wine to the medley of herbs and vegetables. Cook at a brisk pace as you stir vigorously for 3 or 4 minutes. Pour all, piping hot, over the open fish in the serving dish. Serve with green lentils and a potato or chestnut purée.

RED SNAPPER BAKED WITH VEGETABLES

This very popular fish was until recently hardly known to British fishmongers. Both the large and small snappers are particularly suitable for baking and braising.

SERVES 4

4 red snappers, about 7 oz/220 g each	*juice of 1 lemon*
For baking	*a choice of vegetables from the following: small potatoes, whole small onions, baby carrots or large ones sliced, turnips, sweet peppers, courgettes, cauliflower florets*
2 good pinches ground allspice	
2 good pinches ground ginger	
2 good pinches ground cumin	
¼ pt/150 ml olive oil	

Blend the spices with the olive oil and lemon. Boil your selection of, say, four vegetables, separately and gently for 10 minutes each. Drain them and set aside to cool a little. Then brush them over with the spiced oil mixture. Place the vegetables in a circle around the baking dish.

Brush the snappers, inside and out, with the same mixture as that used on the vegetables, and place them in the centre of the baking dish. Set to cook in the oven at gas 6/400°F/200°C for 20 minutes. Test with a sharp-pointed knife at the backbone, to confirm. By this time the vegetables should be completely cooked, and pleasantly browned at the edges. Serve in the baking dish.

FRESH TUNA SWEET AND SOUR

The tuna is an oil-rich fish, very firm in texture, and goes further than most other fish; it needs no heavy, rich sauce to accompany it. It is at its best as here, where a marinade, with a small addition, becomes the sauce.

SERVES 6

2 lb/1 kg tuna, in small fillets or divided steaks

For the marinade

1 tablespoon Spanish or other onion juice

1 teaspoon soy sauce

1 teaspoon honey or sugar

1 tablespoon wine vinegar

juice of 1 lemon

2 bruised bay leaves

3 tablespoons olive oil

1 teaspoon finely ground black pepper

For the sauce

1 tablespoon tomato purée

1/4 pt/150 ml dry red wine

Blend together the marinade ingredients and lay the fish in the marinade in a dish that just fits. Turn the fillets or steaks over from time to time, for a period of half an hour. Then remove them from the marinade and put them in a baking dish in which they fit in a single layer.

Bake in an oven preheated to gas 6/400°F/200°C. Baste with the marinade if necessary. They will take 12-15 minutes, depending on the thickness of the fish, turning them once at half time. This should see them cooked. Remove the fillets or steaks to a covered serving dish, to keep hot.

Now put the marinade in a saucepan, and add to it the tomato purée and the dry red wine. Cook briskly for 4 minutes. Remove the bay leaves, spoon the mixture over the tuna fish, and serve.

VARIATION

Salmon fillets and steaks also respond well to this sweet and sour treatment.

COOKING AU GRATIN

The gratin shows a lovely upper crust when successfully produced. Simple gratins are easily made. It is a useful method of serving fillets, steaks or other cuts of fish poached to a point just before they are fully cooked, and then masked with a sauce that will brown quickly under sharp heat. Thickish butter sauces, sprinkled with breadcrumbs are good for this purpose, but the obvious sauce to use here is the mornay (p. 33). Even when the fish masked by the sauce is already fully cooked, the speed at which the sauce acquires its lovely crust under a fierce grill should enable the dish to be a success. This is another method for regular use in dressing fish.

What is called a 'full gratin' is not quite so simple. In this, uncooked fish is combined in a dish with a sauce which must itself cook and thicken with the fish and its juices, at the same time acquiring that splendid upper crust; and all this is to be done in the oven.

PAUPIETTES OF SOLE FLORENTINE AU GRATIN

Stuffed fillets of Dover sole: this is one of the best ways of serving this fine flavoured and firm textured fish. Here, sandwiched between two layers of savoury spinach, it makes, with the addition of grated cheese and breadcrumbs, a splendid gratin.

SERVES 6

six 4 oz/125 g fillets of Dover sole, with the white skin left on

For the stuffing

2 teaspoons olive oil

5 small mushrooms, chopped

2 shallots, finely chopped

1 anchovy fillet, pounded

1 tablespoon of fine white breadcrumbs

1 tablespoon tomato purée

1 tablespoon finely chopped basil

2 teaspoons Madeira

5 single drops Tabasco or 1 pinch cayenne pepper

juice of 1 lemon

For the 2 sides of the 'sandwich'

1 lb/500 g cooked and drained spinach

1 tablespoon chopped parsley

1 pinch ground nutmeg

1 pinch ground allspice

½ teaspoon salt

½ teaspoon black pepper

¼ pt/150 ml double cream, thoroughly beaten with 1 whole egg

For the gratin topping

2 oz/50 g fine breadcrumbs

2 oz/50 g soft butter

2 oz/50 g finely grated Parmesan

1 oz/25 g finely grated Gruyère

1 teaspoon made English mustard

First make the stuffing. In the oil, cook the mushrooms and shallots until they begin to take colour.

Add this mixture (a simple duxelles) to all the other ingredients, and blend in a food processor.

Now make the 'sandwich' mixture by adding all the other listed ingredients to the spinach, and blending well.

Lay the fillets, skin side down, on a board, and spread the stuffing evenly over them. Roll them up, and either tie them with thin string or secure them by pinning with a cocktail stick. Line the bottom of a baking dish with half the spinach mixture. Lay the fillets in a row on this bed. Cover with the remaining spinach, making all a nice fit. Cover and put the dish into the middle of a preheated oven (gas 4/350°F/180°C) and cook for 25 minutes. At the end of that time remove the dish from the oven, take off the lid, and with a spatula spread the gratin mixture evenly over the top. Replace in the oven, uncovered this time, and raise the temperature to gas 6/400°F/200°C, for a further 12 minutes.

Serve separately a butter and wine sauce.

Note: this recipe for Dover sole starts as an almost dry braise, and only becomes a gratin in its final uncovered stage where it takes on a fine colour.

BEURRE BLANC

2 shallots, finely chopped

3 fl oz/75 ml white wine

3 fl oz/75 ml white wine vinegar

8 oz/250 g unsalted butter

good pinches of salt and finely ground black pepper

In a saucepan, cook the shallots in the wine and vinegar, and reduce to 2 tablespoonfuls. Strain through a conical sieve into another pan, and on low heat beat in the butter, in small nuts, one by one, until it is all absorbed and the sauce looks like well whipped cream. Taste, and season with salt and pepper if necessary. This sauce is one of the most delicate in flavour, and is best used with all good non-oily fish.

FILLETS OF MONKFISH AU GRATIN

SERVES 4

four 6 oz/175 g ½ in/1 cm thick cuts of monkfish, dusted with ½ oz/15 g flour and then shaken

For the sauce

1 tablespoon olive oil

4 oz/125 g finely chopped mushrooms

4 oz/125 g finely chopped onion

1 oz/25 g plain flour

1 pt/600 ml fish stock (p. 30)

4 oz/125 g tomato purée

2 tablespoons red wine

1 tablespoon finely chopped fennel leaves

1 tablespoon finely chopped parsley

1 tablespoon finely chopped basil

pinch of pepper and salt

pinch of ground cumin

2 oz/50 g fresh breadcrumbs

Lay the fillets dusted with flour in a shallow baking dish that will comfortably hold them and 1 pt/600 ml of sauce. Set aside. Into a small saucepan, put the oil. Add the onions and mushrooms, and cook on low heat until they begin to take colour. Remove the pan from the heat and stir in the flour. Replace on the heat, and moisten the mixture with half the fish stock. Stir vigorously, and allow to cook for 1 minute. Now – off the fire again – put in the tomato purée, and again loosen the mixture with the rest of the fish stock and the wine. Add the fennel, parsley, basil, pepper, salt, and the pinch of ground cumin. Mix all well together and pour over the floured fish in the dish. Put the dish in the oven (gas 5/375°F/190°C) for 20 minutes. Remove and sprinkle with the breadcrumbs. Now raise the oven heat to gas 7/425°F/220°C, and allow 5 minutes for the oven to be stabilized at the higher setting. Return the dish to the oven for 10 minutes.

5
BRAISING

Grilling, poaching and baking are quite clear-cut techniques of fish cookery. Braising, a process invented for the slow cooking of the tougher cuts of meat, would appear to have no proper place in fish cookery, where toughness hardly exists. Any whole fine firm fish of impressive size, however, repays the trouble of braising it, and I have chosen some of the handsomest fish for these recipes.

The fish is cooked with vegetables and herbs and a small quantity of liquid, which is reduced or thickened at the end of cooking to make a sauce. Braising allows the flavour of the fish and the vegetables and aromatics to blend thoroughly.

COOKING 'KLEFTIKO' OR EN PAPILLOTE

The 'kleftiko' or 'thieves' kitchen' method of cooking originated in ancient times when outlaws and poachers would cook their wrapped meats in sealed earth-covered ovens, so that no smoke or scent should betray their whereabouts. With the advent of high-quality foil, this form of cooking has made a strong bid to supersede both poaching and braising.

Clearly it is a sensible and clean way of cooking large fish without having to make stock separately. With smaller fish too, and small cuts of firm fish, these silver parcels impart a spirit of present-giving

to the occasion. The way each person unwraps the fishy gift and greets the first scents is an entertainment in itself.

I have found problems in establishing cooking times for these fish parcels for, once they generate internal steam, cooking can be faster than in the poaching process, and what is more, can go on for a considerable time after they have been removed from the oven.

Soft fish, however excellent, are not recommended for this form of cooking. I shall only give, therefore, a tentative recipe for dealing with a 6 oz/175 g steak of any firm fish en papillote.

For inclusion in the parcel with the fish: a choice of either 2 tablespoons of any of the relishes for which a pattern is given on p. 16 or 2 oz/50 g of any of the savoury butters for which a similar pattern is given on p. 18.

Wrap the steak and its accompaniments in a parcel as airtight as you can contrive. Assign to the oven preheated to gas 4/350°F/180°C for 10 minutes. Inspect for any sign of activity within. If such activity is observed, leave it for another 2 minutes, if none, leave longer. Then remove it and transfer the contents to a heated plate.

SALMON TROUT EN PAPILLOTTE

Following the normal procedure for this kind of cookery, we are left, when the fish is cooked, with a residue in the foil of juices of the fish itself and whatever we have put into the parcel ourselves, to begin with.

Using this residue, *soi-même* sauces (p. 19) can be quickly made while the fish is kept covered and warm in the bottom of an oven set at gas 1/275°F/ 140°C, or less. This recipe shows the sort of thing that can be done.

SERVES 6

one 2 lb/1 kg salmon trout

6 scrupulously clean, unopened mussels

1 tablespoon finely chopped celery heart

1 bay leaf

1 tablespoon white wine vinegar

1 tablespoon medium-dry white wine

juice of ½ lemon

pinch of ground allspice

½ teaspoon salt

For the sauce

the strained residues from the foil in which the fish has been cooked

2 egg yolks, beaten up well with 7 fl oz/200 ml double cream

2 oz/50 g softened butter

For garnish

a small bunch of watercress

8 pitted black olives

Make up a foil parcel containing the whole salmon trout, the mussels and all the other ingredients. Close it tightly to ensure nothing leaks out. Place the parcel on a baking tray in the middle of a pre-heated oven (gas 4/350°F/180°C) for 35 minutes. Remove from the oven. Allow the parcel to 'settle down' for a minute. Then open it.

Lift out the trout and put it into a covered serving dish to keep warm at the bottom of a low oven. Set the mussels aside.

In making the sauce, speed is now of the essence. Strain the residues in the foil into a saucepan, and boil quickly to reduce by a third. Remove from the heat and allow to drop well below boiling point. (A cube of ice comes in handy here.) Now beat in the egg and cream mixture over very low heat or in a bain-marie. Continue to beat as you fold in the butter. Beat until the sauce starts to thicken. Remove from fire and keep hot.

Retrieve the trout from the oven. Open it down the back and extract the main bone. Garnish the fish with a few tablespoons of the sauce and decorate with the olives, mussels and sprigs of watercress. Serve the rest of the sauce separately.

Note: the very special cachet given by the mussels, which open inside the foil package to disgorge their marvellous juices, justifies that modest bivalve's claim to be 'the truffle of the sea'.

GREY MULLET BRAISED WITH SORREL AND LETTUCE

If you can't get sorrel, you can substitute spinach, or make the dish just with lettuce, but the flavour will be less good.

SERVES 4

1 grey mullet weighing about 2 lb/1 kg

1 cos lettuce

8 oz/250 g sorrel

2 oz/50 g butter

2 shallots, finely chopped

¼ pt/150 ml dry vermouth

6 tablespoons double cream

salt and pepper

Wash the lettuce, drain well and shred it finely. Wash and drain the sorrel and remove stalks. Heat the butter in an ovenproof dish that will hold the fish comfortably and cook the shallots gently for 5 minutes. Add the shredded lettuce and the sorrel and cook, stirring from time to time, until the lettuce has wilted.

Spread out the vegetables to make a bed for the fish and season with salt and pepper. Put the fish into the dish and pour over the vermouth. Cover with a lid or a well-fitting piece of foil and transfer to a pre-heated oven gas 5/375°F/190°C for 30 minutes.

Remove from the oven, put the mullet on a warmed serving dish and surround with the greens. Keep warm.

Strain the cooking liquid into a pan and boil for a few minutes to reduce somewhat. Lower the heat, stir in the cream and pour the sauce over the fish. Serve at once.

SWORDFISH BRAISED IN TOMATO SAUCE

SERVES 4

4 swordfish steaks, about 1 in/2.5 cm thick

3 tablespoons olive oil

3 cloves garlic, finely chopped

1 large onion, finely chopped

1 1/2 lb/750 g tomatoes, peeled, seeded and chopped

salt and pepper

bouquet garni

juice of 1/2 lemon

Heat the oil in a large pan, add the onion and garlic and cook for a few minutes, then put in the tomatoes. Stew gently for 15 minutes. Put in the swordfish steaks, season all with salt and pepper and tuck in the bouquet garni. Add a little water, if necessary, so that the fish is barely covered.

Cover the pan tightly and braise in a preheated oven, gas 4/350°F/180°C for 25 minutes or until the fish is cooked. Transfer the fish to a serving dish and keep warm. If the sauce looks a little thin, boil for a few minutes to reduce it. Discard the bouquet garni. Stir in the lemon juice, pour the sauce over the fish and serve.

BRAISED SEA BASS IN A VELOUTE SAUCE

This recipe enables us to produce in one pot the court-bouillon for the fish to cook in, the fish stock with which the velouté sauce is made, and the garnish for the fish. It also demonstrates that valuable technique, the blending together of flour and butter (beurre manié) for binding and thickening a strong fish stock and producing, as it were in reverse, a splendid fish velouté sauce.

SERVES 8-10

1 sea bass approximately 4-5 lb/2 kg

For braising

a court-bouillon made according to the following recipe:

5 pt/3 litres water

½ pt/300 ml red or white dry wine

4 roughly chopped whites of leek

4 medium-sized carrots, cut into long strips

4 or 5 medium-sized onions, cut in half

For the sauce

1½ pt/900 ml liquid from the fish kettle

3 oz/75 g softened butter

3 oz/75 g plain flour

4 celery hearts, cut in strips lengthways

2 green peppers, deseeded and cut into strips

2 red peppers, deseeded and cut into strips

2 cloves of garlic, crushed

1 teaspoon ground black pepper

1 teaspoon salt

1 teaspoon ground allspice

3 bouquets garnis

For garnish

quarters of lemon

Put all the ingredients for the court-bouillon into a small fish kettle and cook together for 20 minutes. There should then be still enough liquid to cover the vegetables. Remove from the heat, and allow to cool and the ingredients to infuse. Set oven to gas 3/ 325°F/170°C. Now move the vegetables and herbs to the sides of the tray of the fish kettle, making room for the fish in the middle. The liquid should come up to a third of the depth of the fish. Put on a low heat, cover and bring slowly to simmering point. Unless the fish is very cold, this should not take long. As soon as simmering begins, heap the vegetables around the fish, but not so as to cover it entirely. Cover the kettle tightly and put it in the preheated oven. After 4 minutes, check to see that it is simmering gently. Replace lid closely, and cook for 25 minutes. Now remove the kettle from the oven, and lift out the tray of fish and vegetables slowly, so that the liquid drains back into the kettle. Reserve the liquid. Slide the fish onto a wide, heated serving dish, arranging the strips of vegetables around it and removing the bouquets garnis. Cover to keep hot.

To make the sauce: ladle 1½ pt/900 ml of the braising liquid into a saucepan and cook over low heat. Blend the butter and flour together and when the liquid comes to the boil, drop the flour and butter mixture, little by little, into it until it begins to thicken. Continue the process until you have a good thick velouté sauce.

Keep the sauce hot while with a sharp knife you cut the fish open down the back. Open it out wide on the dish and extract the main bone. Spoon the sliced vegetables over the top of the very white flesh, and take to the table. Serve the sauce separately. Garnish the dish with quarters of lemon.

A hazard of this style of cooking is the uncertainty of braising time in the oven, for if the simmering stops, then the fish probably will not be cooked in the time stated. One cannot keep taking the lid off to inspect every 2 or 3 minutes, but testing after the first 4 minutes is advised.

BRAISED HUSS TANANARIVE

Good firm non-oily fish of the smaller shark family
have, over recent years, become deservedly popular.
Fillets of huss, tope, dogfish and catfish have always
been fine eating when, fried in deep fat at the fried-
fish shop, they were all lumped together under the
one, unnecessarily deceptive, name of 'rock salmon'. These firm fish, full of the flavour of the sea,
are particularly good when treated as in the preced-
ing recipe: braised in a good wine stock and accompanied by a sauce made from the juice of the fish as
it cooks. The following recipe can be applied to all
four of the fish named above, and indeed to any firm
non-oily fish.

SERVES 4-6

2 lb/1 kg thickly cut pieces of huss	*3 sprigs of parsley*
2 pt/1.2 litres of court-bouillon	*1 teaspoon salt*
	1 teaspoon ground black pepper
For the court-bouillon	**For the sauce**
2 pt/1.2 litres water	*3 oz/75 g beurre manié (p. 15)*
¼ pt/150 ml white wine	
1 grated carrot	*12 finely ground green peppercorns*
2 chopped onions	
1 chopped celery heart	*1 tablespoon finely chopped parsley*
1 clove garlic, crushed	

For dealing with these cuts of firm fish we do not
need a large vessel, such as a fish kettle, but rather
the smallest lidded pan which will accept them
loosely packed together, leaving room for as much
court-bouillon as will barely cover them and yet supply enough liquid for a fine strongly flavoured sauce
when braising is done. There is room for nice judge-
ment here.

Boil all the ingredients for the court-bouillon for
25 minutes. Allow to stand, uncovered, and get
cool. Put the pieces of fish in the braising pan,
loosely packed together. When the stock is cool,
strain it onto the fish, and shake the pan so that the
liquid settles down into the crevices. The liquid
should be enough barely to cover the top surfaces of
the fish. Retain any surplus stock for later use in a
sauce or a soup. Set the oven to gas 3/325°F/160°C.
On top of the cooker, bring the stock to simmering
point. Cover, and transfer to the preheated oven.
After 2 minutes, check to see that the stock is still
simmering. Put the cover back and allow to cook for
8 minutes. Then transfer the pan to the top of the
stove, and allow to stand, covered, for 5 minutes.
Remove the pieces of fish to a hot, deep serving dish
and keep warm.

There should now be at least 1 pt/600 ml of rich
fish stock in the pan. Bring this to the boil, and drop
in the beurre manié, piece by piece, stirring vigorously. When the liquid begins to thicken, reduce the
heat and add, first the finely ground green peppercorns and, one minute later, the finely chopped
parsley. Stir well. Pour the hot sauce over the fish in
the deep serving dish. Serve with thoroughly
drained spinach and well buttered mashed potatoes.

6
FRYING

The essentials to the method are good clean oil and a sound fresh batter. I prefer olive oil, but any good groundnut or sunflower oil, would be suitable for frying.

DEEP FRYING

I blame the addiction of the public to deep frying in batter for much of the present almost hostile attitude towards fish in general, and towards the cooking of it at home in particular. If cooking oil is used over and over again, and stale small fragments of fish or batter remain in it, it produces a nauseating odour which has absolutely no connection with fresh fish or good oil. That said, those cooks prepared to take the trouble should not be denied a very valuable and flavour-retaining method of cooking small whole fish, fillets, cuts and steaks of every kind.

Fish for deep frying: especially suited to deep frying in batter are fillets of cod, coley, fresh haddock, lemon sole, plaice and whiting.

To deep fry whitebait, those delicious nurslings of many different types of fish, no batter is required. They should simply be shaken up in a bag with a small quantity of flour. Removed from the bag, they should be tumbled about to dislodge surplus flour and then committed to the hot frying basket.

BASIC BATTER

MAKES ENOUGH TO COVER 4 SERVINGS OF FISH

2 oz/50 g plain flour	*a pinch of salt*
1 whole egg	*¼ pt/150 ml fresh milk*

Put the flour in a bowl. Make a hollow in the middle and put in the egg. With a wooden spoon, stir round and round so that the egg gradually mixes with the flour and both are well blended together and smooth. Then add the salt, and pour in the milk gradually, blending it in. Leave batter to stand for 30 minutes or so before using. When the fish, coated in batter, goes into the basket of the deep-frying pan, the temperature of the oil should be between 312°F/150°C and 325°F/160°C. Test with a small piece of bread which should swiftly turn a pale brown, but get no darker. Most fish deep fried in batter will rise to the surface when cooked. Scoop them out with a perforated slice and drain on kitchen paper. Do not crowd the pan with too many pieces of fish.

SHALLOW FRYING

A much smaller quantity of oil is needed in shallow frying; in an ordinary frying pan it should only come half way up the thickness of the fish being cooked. Fillets of all the fish mentioned above under Deep Frying, except whitebait, are better and more conveniently cooked in this way, first on one side, then on the other. The fillets should be dipped in seasoned beaten egg, then rolled in breadcrumbs, before they are put in the pan of hot oil.

A NOTE ON SAUCES FOR FRIED FISH

The relish (p. 16) is an ingrained habit and not a bad one: a glance back will refresh your memory of the variety of these and the speed with which they can be put together. However, I favour the following classic sauces which, made before frying begins, immediately turn our fried-fish dinner into a gourmet feast: gribiche (p. 31), tartare (p. 32), béarnaise (p. 34), hollandaise (p. 20).

FRYING A LA MEUNIERE

Cooking à la meunière is not only by far the best method of frying, but also one of the best ways of all of cooking fish. Briefly, it is the quick light frying of fillets or whole flat fish, dusted with flour, in really hot butter. When the fish is cooked on both sides, it is removed from the pan, to which more butter is added and then swirled around until foaming. The juice of half a lemon is then introduced, together with a tablespoon of finely chopped parsley. This piping hot mixture is poured over the fish, which has been kept hot in a heated serving dish. The only sauce needed is the butter.

PLAICE A LA MEUNIERE

SERVES 4

four 6 oz/175 g fillets of plaice

1 oz/25 g plain flour

4 oz/125 g unsalted butter

2 pinches ground black pepper

2 pinches of salt

juice of 1 lemon

2 tablespoons finely chopped parsley

1 lemon, quartered

Brush the fillets of plaice with flour. Shake well to remove any surplus. Put 2 oz/50 g unsalted butter in the pan, and when hot, put the fillets in to cook. After 3 minutes, turn them over, and cook for a further 3 minutes. Remove them to a heated serving dish. Now put the rest of the butter into the pan with the seasonings. Stir all around until the hot butter begins to foam. Pour in the lemon juice, down the side of the pan, and add the parsley. Stir all around, and pour piping hot over the fillets in the serving dish. Serve with quarters of lemon.

Note: for all cooking à la meunière, unsalted or clarified butter is essential as, although it should become nut-brown when very hot, it should not be allowed to burn. The addition of a teaspoon of oil at the earliest stage of the frying helps to avoid subsequent burning, and does not invalidate the recipe.

VARIATION

Use lemon or Torbay sole instead of plaice.

FRITTO MISTO

For this simple 'fry-up', it is best to choose from
either fillets of all firm fish, such as sole, turbot, brill
and monkfish, or all soft fish, such as plaice, cod,
hake, lemon sole, haddock, so that all the fish will
be cooked at roughly the same rate. In this recipe,
firm fish is used.

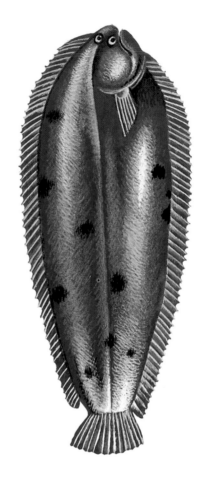

SERVES 4-6

6 oz/175 g fillet of sole

6 oz/175 g fillet of brill

6 oz/175 g fillet of
monkfish

4 scallops

4 large cooked prawns

sufficient oil to cover the
frying pan to the depth of
¼ in/5 mm

5 fl oz/150 ml batter
(p. 50)

4 oz/125 g small
mushrooms, quartered by
cutting down through the
stalks twice

1 tablespoon finely
chopped parsley

For the sauce

3 tablespoons olive or nut
oil

1 clove garlic, crushed

2 shallots, finely chopped

1 lb/500 g peeled
tomatoes, finely chopped

salt and pepper

To garnish

lemon segments

Make the sauce first. In the pan, sweat the garlic and
shallots in the oil until they are soft. Add the tomatoes, salt and pepper, and cook vigorously until all
becomes a thickish purée. Set aside, and keep hot.

Cut the fillets of fish into 1 oz/25 g pieces. Bisect
the scallops horizontally through the white flesh.
Separate the coral 'cock's combs'. Peel and bisect the
prawns, head to tail. Set the scallop and prawn
pieces aside until the fillets have been cooked. Roll
the pieces of fish in the batter, and let them stand for
10 minutes. Meanwhile, heat the oil in the pan until
it is almost smoking. Put in the fish, and cook until

nicely browned on both sides. Remove them, using
a perforated slice, to a warm serving dish. Cover and
keep them warm in the bottom of a low oven. Now,
having removed any particles of singed batter from
the oil remaining in the pan, toss in the pieces of
mushroom and shellfish, and move them around for
3 minutes. Take the pan from the heat, and scatter
the parsley over all. Retrieve the fried fish pieces
from the oven, and pour the contents of the pan over
them. Make a space in the middle of the dish into
which the thick tomato sauce can now be poured.
Adorn the rim of the dish with segments of lemon.

7
SHELLFISH
& CEPHALOPODS

My arbitrary separation, up to now, of the round and flat fish from their marine cousins and collaterals, the shellfish – under which term I include all shellfish from the crustacea-like lobster to the winkle we eat with a pin – requires some explanation.

Under self-imposed sumptuary laws and in a sincere missionary spirit, I have withheld from the sauce recipes given so far – which usually provide the names for the dishes with which they are served – that enrichment first with egg yolks, cream and butter, then with garnishes of shellfish and other expensive delicacies – which would entitle them to awesome menu names, such, for instance as the following, which demand for garnish, after the egg yolk, cream and butter enrichment: *Nantua*, poached oysters and slices of truffles; *Normande*, poached oysters and mussels, prawns, shrimps, gudgeons, crayfish and croûtons; *Daumont*, mushrooms with a chop-up or *salpicon* of crayfish bound with *Sauce Nantua*, quenelles of fish forcemeat, slices of soft roes egged-and-breadcrumbed and fried; *Cardinal*, slices of lobster tails combined with slices of truffle.

I hope that the home cook, having mastered the simple classic sauces, will now be tempted to try some of these grander versions.

Shellfish offer an explosion of sensations for the eye and the palate as we enter the rococo haunts of the lobster, the crawfish, the crab and the prawn, the sandy lurking places of the scallop, the shrimp and the multitudinous cockle, and the seaweed covered rocky retreats of the mussel.

LOBSTER

I suppose that for some people this blue-black grandee of the deep is an everyday dish. To me it is an increasingly rare feast, and stirs up memories of youthful extravagance. Those who do buy lobster will usually buy them freshly boiled but shoppers who buy them live should kill them by sudden immersion in boiling water; this kills them instantly.

Cooking times: a lobster weighing 1 lb/500 g will be cooked after 15 minutes' boiling. For every additional 1 lb/½ kg add 10 minutes.

ALAN
CRACKNELL

LOBSTER MORNAY

SERVES 4

two 1 lb/500 kg freshly boiled lobsters

1½ pt/900 ml mornay sauce (p. 33)

1 tablespoon Madeira, Muscatel or Port wine

1 teaspoon made mustard

Split the lobsters into four half-shells. Remove the black thread of intestine from the end of the tail and the sac from the head parts. Take the lobster meat out of the tails and claws, and dice it. Now scoop out the soft and green edible parts from the heads, and in a small bowl moisten them with the wine and the mustard, and mix thoroughly together. Brush the lobster meat over with this mixture. Next, put 2 tablespoons of the mornay sauce in the bottom of each shell. Put back the lobster meat, and cover with the rest of the sauce. Put under a brisk grill to brown. Ten minutes should be enough.

LOBSTER THERMIDOR

SERVES 4

two 1 lb/500 g freshly boiled lobsters

½ pt/300 ml bercy sauce (p. 25)

½ pt/300 ml béchamel sauce (p. 19)

2 teaspoons made mustard

Proceed as in the previous recipe, but do not dice the tail meat, which should be extracted whole, cut with a sharp knife into fine slices, and then put back, as if intact, into the shells, which have been previously moistened with a few tablespoons of the two sauces. Now crack the claws and extract the flaky meat, and put it in a bowl with the green and soft parts scooped from the head. Add the mustard, and mix all well together. Next, with a teaspoon, separate each slice of the tail meat and put in some of the mixture. Cover with the remaining sauces, thoroughly combined, and brown lightly under the grill.

Note: observe the differing use of mustard in this and the former recipe. In the first case the mustard is there simply to give a flavour. In the second, it is meant to sting a little.

LOBSTER IN COQUILLES

Although we cannot afford to eat lobster often, a lot can be done with one small lobster in mixed fish dishes, the best of which are coquilles: those served in shell-shaped dishes. The presence and flavour of lobster enhance a mix of small poached fillets of firm, non-oily fish, such as monk, sole, turbot. Covered in a good sauce, and put under the grill or in a hot oven for a few minutes, coquilles make splendid lunch and supper dishes.

The deep conch shell of the scallop is best for these confections, in which the scallop itself can play a major part, as, of course, can mussels. Do ask the fishmonger for both shells of this beautiful bivalve, do not be content with the flat shell on which they are usually displayed. Deep scallop conch shells should be collected like fine china, and kept as scrupulously clean and unchipped. (Besides, they are the prettiest of serving dishes, for a large number of poultry, meat and vegetable dishes in general cookery.)

MIXED FISH COQUILLE DISHES

These savoury confections are useful in enabling the cook to make the most of small quantities of lobster (or crawfish or large prawns) by 'stretching' them with other fish, without obliterating the unique flavour and texture of those expensive crustacea. The selection of fish to be included will be guided by the cook's inclination and budget. The following recipe includes two different kinds of fish, apart from the lobster, and will give a flavour of lobster throughout.

COQUILLE OF LOBSTER TANANARIVE

SERVES 6

1 lb/500 g poached fillets of haddock (or whiting, plaice, coley)

8 oz/250 g poached monkfish or angler tail

1 lb/500 g lobster, cooked

1/2 pt/300 ml thick cream

2 teaspoons chives, finely chopped

1 tablespoon ground green peppercorns

1 teaspoon horseradish cream

1/2 teaspoon ground cloves

2 teaspoons muscatel or other sweet dessert wine

salt to season

1 1/2 lb/750 g cooked potato, mashed with 3 oz/ 75 g of butter and 1 whole egg and 1 egg yolk beaten into it

For serving

6 large scallop shells (or cocottes) 4 in/10 cm in diameter and 2 in/5 cm deep

---

Flake the haddock, and cut up the monkfish into small pieces (1/2 oz/15 g), and set aside. Cut the lobster open, head to tail. Remove the black intestine, and extract the inedible sac from the head. Spoon out from the head all the green and soft edible parts, and put them in a mixing-bowl. Set aside.

Extract all the flesh from the tail and claws. Cut up the tail meat into very fine slices, and quarter these. Flake the claw meat, and set all aside. Now pour the cream into the bowl containing the green and soft edible parts from the lobster head, and beat well together. Add all the herbs and spices, and wine, and blend together in a homogenous mixture.

Put 2 or 3 tablespoons of the mashed potato into the bottom of each scallop shell, and pat down gently. On top of each, put 3 heaped tablespoons of the flaked and chopped fish, and press it down flat. Add to each a tablespoon of the enriched thick cream, and spread it over the fish. Add more potato, then more fish, and again more cream, and so on, until the flaked fish is all used.

The scallops should now be two-thirds full, and there should still be enough of the enriched cream to moisten all the lobster flesh, stirred around in it in the bowl. Distribute the lobster meat evenly in the 6 shells, and press it down flat. The balance of the potato can now be put in to fill completely and make a mound on top of each shell. Put the shells on a baking tray into the middle of a preheated oven (gas 4/350°F/180°C) for 20-25 minutes. Serve with a beurre blanc (p. 43) or a hollandaise sauce (p. 20).

COLD LOBSTER

Cook the lobsters, if bought live as described on p. 54; split in half and clean as in Lobster Mornay (p. 56). Serve at room temperature, not chilled.

SAUCES FOR COLD LOBSTER

Most cold fish (and this is especially true of shellfish, and of lobster, crawfish, prawns and crab) lose much of their flavour when served at refrigerator temperature. It should be a rule therefore that, before serving such cold dishes, they should be allowed to reach at least a reasonable living-room temperature before they are brought to table. The same rule applies to the mayonnaise and other sauces and the salads which accompany the fish.

These following sauces all go well with cold dishes of lobster and other shellfish.

Mayonnaise (p. 21) and all the sauces derived from it, the following being perhaps the most approved by custom and acclaim:

Remoulade sauce: into ½ pt/300 ml mayonnaise work 1 teaspoon French mustard and 1 pounded anchovy fillet. Then fold in 2 teaspoons each of finely chopped pickled gherkin, parsley, capers, basil and tarragon.

Escoffier mayonnaise: into ½ pt/300 ml mayonnaise fold 1 teaspoon creamed horseradish and 1 teaspoon each of finely chopped parsley, chervil and chives.

Tartare sauce: see p. 32.

Green sauce: to ½ pt/300 ml mayonnaise, add 1 teaspoon of each of the following, all finely chopped and pounded: watercress, chervil, blanched young spinach leaf, fresh tarragon and chives. (Fresh basil can be substituted for the tarragon to make a fresher-tasting sauce.)

These are the best known mayonnaise sauces, but there remain many variants to be developed by the use of relishes, reduced to a spoonful or two of concentrated flavour, which can then be worked into the egg yolk before the oil is beaten in (p. 16).

Apart from mayonnaise, the sauce I recommend for frequent use is the gribiche (p. 31), made with hard-boiled egg yolks. Not to be despised for its simplicity is the range of vinaigrettes (p. 21).

CRAWFISH, PRAWNS, SHRIMPS
SCAMPI (DUBLIN BAY PRAWNS)

The crawfish can be treated just as lobster, though it is short of the lovely claw meat of the latter. However, crawfish and all the other crustaceans mentioned above are expensive as the main ingredient of a meal. It is only good sense to combine very small quantities of these expensive fish with others to make mixed fish dishes, such as pilafs, salads, soufflés, soups and pies, where their pronounced individual flavours will still come through. Recipes of this nature will be found later in the book, and will indicate the possibility for the home cook to economise while still occasionally indulging and – I hope – expanding appreciation of the good things that come from the sea.

CRAB

Formerly, like the oyster, the mussel and the scallop, one of the few privileges of the poor, the stereotyped dressed crab of the English 'Margate' tradition provides splendid nutritional value. However, I believe it is still regarded as a holiday treat; part of periodical visits to the seaside, but not a regular feature in home menus. This is a pity because the British crab is better flavoured and much meatier than those usually met with at Costa This and Costa That abroad.

For those unfamiliar with the crab, the fishmonger will willingly demonstrate how to open it and remove the few inedible parts. The cracking of the claws and the extraction of their meat takes a little time but is not unpleasant, and the dressing of the meat provides endless scope for happy experiment.

Cooking live crabs: If you buy live crabs, make sure the big claws are tied, to prevent any annoying nips as you try to get them out of the bag when you get home. As with the lobster, the best way of killing a crab is to drop it quickly into a pan of boiling water. For crabs weighing between 1 lb/500 g and 2 lb/1 kg, boil hard for 3 or 4 minutes, and then simmer for a further 8 to 10 minutes. Crabs weighing 2 lb/1 kg and over will require, after an initial fierce boiling of 4 minutes, a further 12 to 14 minutes' simmering.

DRESSED CRAB

A crab of 1 lb/500 g to 1½ lb/750 g is a very full and filling meal for one. This recipe which departs from the English stereotype of crabmeat bulked out with breadcrumbs and then sprinkled with vinegar, salt and pepper, will be found to be something of an improvement.

SERVES 4

four 1 lb/500 g freshly cooked crabs

1 pt/600 ml thick béchamel sauce (p. 19)

4 oz/125 g of a selected savoury butter (p. 18 and below)

1 tablespoon finely chopped parsley

optional: fine breadcrumbs, finely grated Parmesan or other cheese sufficient to sprinkle thinly over each serving

For savoury butter
suggested ingredients, one of which is to be blended, in the quantities given, with 4 oz/125 g butter:

1 teaspoon pounded garlic

2 teaspoons ground green peppers

2 small fillets pounded anchovy

1 teaspoon made mustard

1 teaspoon creamed horseradish

1 teaspoon tomato purée

1 tablespoon finely chopped shallot

1 tablespoon finely chopped capers

1 tablespoon finely chopped celery heart

1 tablespoon finely chopped fennel

Break up the claws and legs of the crabs and extract all the white meat. Now tackle the intricately constructed, bony chine, and extract the white meat from that. Put all the white meat together in one bowl.

Scoop out the brown meat and creamy substances from the shell. If it is summer time, and one or two of your crabs are female, scoop out the lining of red coral from the large shell. Put all this meat, brown and red, into a separate bowl. Reserve and clean the crab shells.

On a low fire, heat up the béchamel sauce, and add the savoury butter of your choice. Stir well as the mingled sauce and butter become really hot. Do not allow to boil. Pour half of this combined mixture into a separate pan.

Put the brown and red meat into one of the pans, and the white meat into the other, in each case mixing the sauce and meat together. Now fill the clean crab shells with alternate tablespoons of white and dark meat till the saucepans are empty. Put on a tray in a preheated oven (gas 5/375°F/190°C) for 10 minutes. Sprinkle with the parsley and serve.

Alternatively, at the penultimate stage, sprinkle the loaded shells with breadcrumbs and Parmesan or other cheese, and put in a hot oven (gas 7/425°F/220°C) for 6 minutes or till brown.

BOILED CRABS FOR A PARTY

Delicious as such sauced crab dishes are, a great deal of happiness can be had by simply placing an opened cooked crab, relieved of its inedibles, in front of each person at the table, and providing whatever you have in the way of nutcrackers, lobster picks, marrow extractors, pickle forks and skewers, as well as a sprinkler bottle containing a good relish (p. 16), paper napkins galore, bottles of good wine, red and/or white, and real bread and butter.

Watch and listen as the claws go crack. Study the varying skills of the protagonists, particularly when they tackle the chine, which contains as much good meat as the claw if only it can be skilfully extruded.

Perhaps this is the best way of all to eat crab; in a jolly company around the table, everyone busy and, in a sense, competitive, though there is no prize to be gained for being the first to exhaust one's crab's resources.

CRAB CURRY

This sauce, hot in both senses, can also be used with other crustacea and any firm fish.

SERVES 4

4 good crabs	2 teaspoons ground coriander
For the curry sauce	
1 small, finely chopped hot red chilli	juice of 1 lemon
	2 teaspoons wine vinegar
2 teaspoons finely grated root ginger	2 tablespoons Madeira, port or full sherry
2 teaspoons ground cumin	½ teaspoon cayenne pepper
2 teaspoons turmeric powder	1 teaspoon salt

Break off the claws of the crab, and extract all the meat, both white and brown. Clean the main shells.

Blend all the ingredients for the sauce in a food processor, and then cook gently in a saucepan, stirring all the time, for 12-15 minutes. Distribute the sauce evenly in the crab shells. Mix the crabmeat together and lay it on top of the sauce. With two forks, turn the contents of the shells over, from the bottom up, so as to obtain a rough mixture of the two elements.

Cover the filled crab shells with foil, and put into a moderate oven (gas 4/350°F/180°C) for 15 minutes. Serve with cumin- and clove-spiced long grained rice, and a chop-up of tomatoes and onions.

MUSSELS

Within these black shells is to be found the concentrated essence and sea-impregnated succulence of seafood at its best. Even the oyster cannot compete – and the oyster is far less useful to the fish cook, losing much of its flavour when cooked. The mussel, on the other hand, improves with the slight cooking it should get: just enough to open it and to dress it. Mussels are excellent uncooked, but much better prepared and treated in their most popular and classic way as moules marinière, my next recipe.

Shopping note: when buying mussels, whether shaggy and barnacle-strewn or clean-shelled, buy a good many more than you estimate you will need. Experience indicates that at least one in ten shells will be open, broken, cracked or filled with mud.

Preparation: scrub the shells well. Pull out the beard or byssus protruding from the centre of the concave edge. Test each mussel by kneading strongly with the fingers. If any substance oozes out, discard. Reject those that are slightly open and do not immediately snap shut when you handle them.

MOULES MARINIERE

SERVES 4

3 lb/1½ kg mussels

½ bottle white wine, not extremely dry

½ pt/300 ml water

1 teaspoon ground black pepper

1 finely chopped shallot

2 sprigs of fennel leaves

4 stalks and heads of parsley

4 tablespoons finely chopped parsley

Into a large two-handled lidded pan put the wine, water, pepper, shallot and sprigs of fennel and parsley. Reserve the chopped parsley. Load in the mussels as gently as possible. Shake them a little, to settle them down evenly. Cover and heat rapidly, to raise steam. Shake the pan and allow 30 seconds' further steaming, before turning off the heat. Lift the lid, and give one more shake, and let the mussels, which will now all be open, stand for a minute, to allow their juices to drain down into the cooking liquid. With a large perforated spoon or ladle, move the mussels to a colander, placed over a bowl to collect any juices still draining from them. Cover with a cloth to keep warm. Now strain the cooking liquid into a smaller, more convenient pan. Add the mussel juices from the bowl under the colander, and heat the liquid, but not to boiling point. Stir in the chopped parsley and remove from the heat. Distribute the mussels in hot soup plates, and pour or ladle the hot liquid over them. One of the great flavours of the world.

VARIATION

Some people prefer a more substantial liquid, and, in another version of the recipe, the cooking liquid is thickened with beurre manié (p. 15) before stirring in the parsley and ladling over the mussels. To thicken ½ pt/300 ml of liquid use ½ oz/15 g beurre manié made of equal proportions of butter and flour.

OTHER WAYS WITH MUSSELS

Having cleaned them and opened them by steaming, there are many ways of dressing mussels, all of them delicious. Put a small pat of any savoury butter (p. 18) on each of a dozen mussels in the half shell, and place them in a moderate oven for a few minutes. Again in the half shell, add a teaspoon of any sauce derived from the fish velouté or the béchamel, and put under a hot grill for a few minutes. And, vice versa, put a few mussels and the strained juices drained from them into any of the classic sauces, and it becomes miraculously transformed and improved. In this way it has played and still plays a tremendous role in the history of fish cooking.

SCALLOPS

Several hundred years after Botticelli so beautifully depicted Venus arising in a scallop shell from the warm middle sea, another Italian, Maître Emilio Boscasso, chef of Hatchett's restaurant in Piccadilly, met a chilly end in the North Atlantic. On his way to benevolent internment in Canada with many other enemy aliens, his ship was torpedoed and sank with all hands.

   The following recipe is by way of a tribute to a friend and one of the most resourceful cooks.

SCALLOPS BOSCASSO

The recipe is a reminder of the ingenuity required to provide adequate meals at controlled prices in a climate of acute shortage. I am glad to reflect that Boscasso helped to raise the lowly scallop to the exalted status it now has in English cooking

SERVES 4

4 large scallops or 8 small ones	1 pt/600 ml béchamel sauce (p. 19)
2 large baked potatoes	melted butter
1 tablespoon olive oil	2 pt/1.2 litres court-bouillon for non-oily fish (p. 28)
1 shallot, finely chopped	
3 oz/75 g mushrooms, finely chopped	

Scoop out the potatoes leaving the skins intact. Brush the outsides of these very thinly with oil (or butter) and let them get crisp in a moderate oven. In the olive oil, in a small pan, cook the finely chopped shallot and mushrooms until they form almost a

purée. Add this mixture to the béchamel sauce.

Meanwhile remove the skirt (ragged edge) and the black, thread-like intestine from the scallops, and poach them gently in the warm court-bouillon for 3-4 minutes. Remove them to a plate, reserving the orange 'cock's combs' for garnish, and chop them up and keep them warm.

Now line the bottom of each potato skin with 2 tablespoons of the enriched béchamel sauce. Lay the chopped scallops over this. Pour over each some of the remaining béchamel sauce, leaving room for a layer of half the original contents of the potato skins, mashed, to be heaped on top. Brush the potato top – patterned with a fork – with melted butter, and put in a hot oven to become a really deep brown. Sprinkle with parsley, and stick one 'cock's comb' upright in the centre of each half potato. To be consumed potato skins and all!

VARIATIONS

This simple recipe can be applied to all other poached fish and shellfish: lobster, sole, monkfish or turbot Boscasso. The crisp potato skin is the feature of the dish; the sauce can be varied at the discretion of the cook.

OTHER SCALLOP SUGGESTIONS

Scallops go well with almost any sauce, particularly with mornay (p. 33) or black butter (p. 25). Sliced horizontally and lightly fried à la meunière, they are delicious.

Although scallops are not quite so pungently reminiscent of the sea as mussels, they can be used to great effect in finishing a sauce or can be served sliced as a garnish for sole, turbot, halibut, brill or monkfish. They are almost essential ingredients of a good fish pie (p. 89).

THE CEPHALOPODS

Octopus, squid, cuttlefish: comparative newcomers to the British scene, these are not only the most nourishing and subtly flavoured of fish but, in the case of the squid and cuttlefish, are the easiest to cook of all the fish we have encountered so far. Their appearance may be intimidating, but they are quite easy to deal with.

The octopus is a tough customer, and unless he has been thoroughly beaten will never really become tender, though the sauce that will come from him, and the vegetables and herbs cooked with him, will be exquisite; to be lapped up eagerly, with chunks of brown bread: a meal in itself. One fishmonger in the town where I live uses a small cement-mixer into which he shovels, with three or four octopus, a couple of spadefuls of flint shingle from the beach, rotating it at full speed: the shingle breaks every sinew in the octopus in about 20 minutes. It is then ready to cook.

Such resources are not usually available to the home cook. When buying octopus, therefore, a shopper should enquire whether it has been already prepared for cooking. If the answer is 'yes' then why not have a go?

To clean a squid or cuttlefish: the best way to prepare these fish for cooking is to cut from the head to the tentacles – to be cooked with the rest of the fish – pull the head and any attachments away from the bag, remove the quill, in the case of the squid, or the chalky oval bone, in the cuttlefish (though these can be much more easily removed when the fish is cooked). Slit the bag at the apex of its closed end. Search for and remove any grit that you find there. The bag and the tentacles are all that is essential to cook, but the head should then be explored surgically to locate the ink-sac, which will almost certainly on a first occasion disclose its presence only too clearly if it is broken into. This ink is an essential part of many recipes. Long familiarity with the squid and the cuttlefish has led me to confine my own preparations to making sure there is no grit lurking at the bottom of the closed end of the bag.

CUTTLEFISH CASSEROLE

This recipe can be used for squid and tenderised octopus as well, but in the case of octopus cooking time should be extended to 1 hour or until tender.

SERVES 4

1½ lb/750 g cuttlefish	1 sprig thyme
8 oz/250 g finely chopped shallots	1 sprig rosemary
4 tablespoons olive oil	3 bay leaves
6 oz/175 g chopped celery	1 lb/500 g peeled tomatoes
4 oz/125 g chopped green pepper	1 pt/600 ml red wine
a good pinch of ground allspice	4 oz/125 g tomato purée

Soften the shallots in the olive oil. Put in the cuttlefish, cut up in pieces, or whole. Move the fish around while it cooks for 12 minutes. Add the celery and the green pepper, and the herbs and spices. Cut up and lay the tomatoes over all, and cook briskly until the tomatoes begin to meld with the other ingredients. Now transfer to an earthenware pot just big enough to hold all these ingredients and the wine and the tomato purée, loosened with a spoonful or two of the wine. Cook in a preheated moderate oven, gas 4/350°F/180°C for about 40 minutes.

A SAUTE OF SQUID

SERVES 5

2 lb/1 kg of squid, preferably small (with ink sacs and 'quills' removed see p. 64)	¼ pt/150 ml olive oil
	juice of ½ lemon
water	salt and black pepper to season
2 tablespoons wine vinegar	

Put the whole squid in a small pan. Add just enough water to cover, and add the vinegar. Bring to the boil and simmer very gently for 45 minutes or until tender. Remove from the heat. Drain, and then cool under a running cold tap. Remove to a plate and cut into small 1 in/2.5 cm pieces or strips.

Heat the olive oil in a frying pan, and gently sauté the squid pieces until very lightly browned. Remove from the oil to a hot dish. Season with salt and pepper and sprinkle with lemon juice. Serve with a dip of rouille (p. 86).

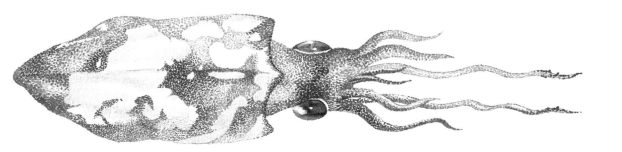

—8—
CURED AND PRESERVED FISH

In Britain we are fortunate to have a wide range of smoked, salted and pickled fish, some prepared for centuries in these islands, others from northern Europe that we have come to know in recent years, readily available from the fishmonger or delicatessen. They range from the luxurious and expensive to simple everyday fare, and all make excellent eating.

Smoked salmon, trout, mackerel and **eel** are all best eaten as they are, with a squeeze of lemon juice or a sprinkle of a relish in which cayenne pepper is mildly present. Serve with them cress or cucumber sandwiches made with thin brown bread and butter.

Kippers are best grilled, brushed with butter and put to a high heat. Watch your kipper as it grills, and the moment the main bone buckles and springs up, it is cooked. Whip it away onto a hot plate. Serve with toast and butter. (One should always remember that a single kipper never seems to be enough.)

The **bloater,** another and remarkable role played by that paragon of fishes, the herring, is as different from the kipper as Danish Blue is from a good strong Cheddar. If you are lucky, you will find a hard roe inside; this, to me, is one of the great delicacies. Bake your bloater, unopened, in the oven (gas 6/ 400°F/200°C) for 10 minutes. Accompaniments: as for kippers.

Smoked haddock is a marvellous exception to the rule that non-oily fish are not improved by smoking. (I have smoked grey mullet with some success, and I believe that large grey mullet are being smoked in the United States today.) There is no doubt that the fresh haddock, a quality fish when fresh, is immeasurably enhanced by smoking. (Smoked cod and coley, and whiting, though gallant challengers, are much better eaten fresh.)

To cook the smoked haddock, put it in a pan and cover with a half and half mixture of milk and water. Bring to simmering point. Allow to cook gently for 3 minutes. Then withdraw the pan from the fire, and allow the fish to complete its cooking in the hot liquid for a further 6 minutes. Remove to a dish and garnish generously with pats of butter.

A recipe for kedgeree with haddock is on p. 90.

Arbroath smokies are small haddock. Brush well with butter and grill for a few minutes.

SOUSED HERRINGS OR MACKEREL

Soused herrings or mackerel are simple to prepare, and a wonderful cold food, accompanied by a potato and watercress salad.

SERVES 6

six 7 oz/225 g fish, cleaned and headless

For the sousing liquid

wine vinegar

1 tablespoon mixed pickling spice

1 teaspoon salt

1 large onion, finely sliced

2 bay leaves

Put the fish in the bottom of a baking dish which accepts them all, side by side. With a measuring jug, pour in water, just to cover the fish then pour in the same amount of wine vinegar, and put in all the other ingredients.

Place the dish in the middle of the oven (gas 1/275°F/140°C) and cook for 2 hours. Allow to cool, and then put in the refrigerator, still in the sousing liquid, till required.

PICKLED HERRINGS OR ROLLMOPS

SERVES 4

8 good-sized herring fillets

For stuffing the fillets

2 pickled gherkins, finely chopped

2 shallots, finely sliced

4 teaspoons chopped capers

For the pickling mixture

1 pt/600 ml wine vinegar

1 tablespoon spirit vinegar

2 shallots, finely sliced

2 tablespoons salt

2 whole cloves

6 black peppercorns, crushed

1 large bay leaf

pinch of cayenne pepper

1 teaspoon sugar

Lay the fillets, skin down, on a flat surface, and cover them with the finely chopped gherkins, shallots and capers. Roll each fillet up tightly, from the tail, and secure the bundles by spiking with half toothpicks. Lay the rollmops so that they fit tightly in a terrine. Pour over them the cold pickling liquid. Cover, and leave in the refrigerator for 4 days.

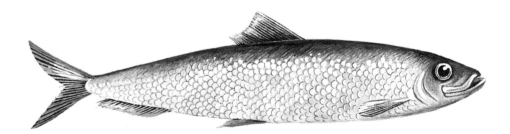

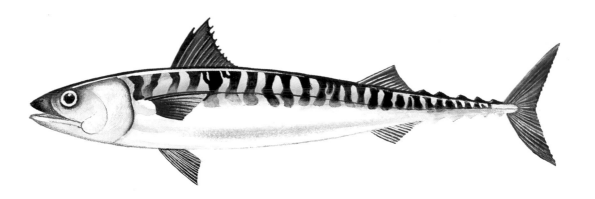

MACKEREL IN WHITE WINE

SERVES 4

4 small or 2 large mackerel	a few black peppercorns
½ bottle dry white wine	1 bay leaf
½ pt/300 ml water	a strip of lemon peel
2 onions, sliced	a sprig of tarragon or a few celery leaves
salt	chopped parsley

Make a court-bouillon: put all the ingredients except the mackerel and parsley into a pan and bring to the boil. Cook steadily until the liquid is reduced by half. Leave to cool.

Clean the fish and put them in a pan. Strain over the court-bouillon and bring slowly to simmering point. Simmer very gently for 5-8 minutes, depending on the size of the fish, then remove the pan from the heat and leave to cool.

Lift out the mackerel, and remove the skin and bones. Place the fillets in a serving dish. Strain the cooking liquid and taste it. If the flavour is not strong enough, reduce the liquid a little more. When it is cool again pour it over the fish.

The mackerel will keep, covered with foil, for several days in the refrigerator. Garnish with chopped parsley before serving.

MARINATED SARDINES

SERVES 6

2 lb/1 kg sardines	4 tablespoons court-bouillon (p. 28) or water
flour	2 sprigs thyme
salt	2 bay leaves
¼ pt/150 ml olive oil	peppercorns
4 cloves garlic, crushed	parsley
¼ pt/150 ml wine vinegar	
¼ pt/150 ml dry white wine	

Clean the fish, but leave on their heads. Dust them with flour mixed with a little salt. Heat 4 tablespoons of the oil and fry the sardines until golden on both sides and cooked through. Remove the sardines to a serving dish and pour the remaining oil into the frying pan. Put in the garlic cloves and fry until they are golden, then add the vinegar, wine, court-bouillon or water, herbs, peppercorns and salt. Boil fiercely for 4-5 minutes to reduce the liquid. Pour over the fish and leave to cool, then cover and refrigerate for at least 3 days. When you are ready to serve the sardines, bring the dish to room temperature, remove the thyme and bay leaves and sprinkle with chopped parsley.

CEVICHE

The method of quick curing or pickling raw fresh salmon, as exemplified in the recipe for Gravlax (p. 71), is simplified in the ceviche. This is a recipe which may be applied to all the best firm fish, among which I would specifically select Dover sole, turbot, brill, halibut, bass, river trout and – among shellfish – the scallop, opened at home and immediately dealt with. Ceviche is a dish which demands the very freshest of fine fish, and calls for a piquant sweet and sour relish, as here, and an accompanying purée of vegetables or a potato salad.

SERVES 6

1½ lb/750 g fillet, cut from a large fresh turbot	1 tablespoon finely chopped capers
For the marinade	2 teaspoons juice from a Spanish onion
½ pt/300 ml lemon juice	
For the relish	2 small anchovy fillets, pounded
¼ pt/150 ml white wine vinegar	**For the garnish**
1 tablespoon muscatel or other dessert wine	6 black olives
	sprigs of parsley

With a sharp knife cut the thick fillet into slices ⅛ in/3 mm thick and of roughly the same size and shape. Pass the slices, one by one, through a bowl containing the lemon juice, and lay them in a shallow dish, leaving a small space between each slice. When the bottom of the dish is covered, put a second layer of slices on top of the first, in much the same way as bricklayers lay bricks. Continue the process until all the slices are in the dish. Cover with lemon juice and put into the refrigerator for 6 hours.

Blend all the ingredients for the relish together, and allow to stand.

When the time comes, remove the fish from the refrigerator and, before serving, allow to stand for sufficient time to attain room temperature. Now drain off any surplus lemon juice. Spoon over the relish and garnish with olives and parsley.

VARIATION

As an alternative to the sweet and sour relish with the ceviche, try the mustard sauce which accompanies Gravlax (p. 71).

Incidentally, schnapps, aquavit or vodka, in short nips, will be found to enliven the scene, though I myself prefer red wine.

GRAVLAX

This authentic Swedish recipe is only one of many variants, and is a quick method of curing the salmon so that it is ready for eating only 12 hours after preparation. The sauce is an essential accompaniment.

SERVES 12

4½-5 lb/2-2½ kg middle cut from a large fresh salmon

4-5 large bunches of dill

For the pickling mixture

3 tablespoons sea salt

3 tablespoons crushed white peppercorns

2 tablespoons caster sugar

1 teaspoon saltpetre, available at chemists

For the sauce

3 fl oz/75 ml water

2 tablespoons of made English mustard

2 teaspoons caster sugar

1 tablespoon wine vinegar

7 fl oz/200 ml olive oil

1 tablespoon finely chopped dill

Blend all the ingredients for the pickling mixture together in a mortar, it being particularly important for the saltpetre to be distributed throughout. Scrape the skin of the salmon well, and fillet the fish from the ventral side without separating the 2 skinned sides when it is open. The filleting, if thorough, will produce many small channels into the salmon flesh. With the hands now rub the pickling mixture well into the exposed flesh. Bruise some bunches of dill, and spread plenty of them over the fish. Now close the fish up, thus restoring the salmon to its original shape. Thickly line an oblong straight-sided dish – one that will just accept the piece of salmon – with more bruised dill. Lay the salmon on this bed, and pack more dill in round the edges, the amount of dill to be used being only limited by the amount that can be packed in. Cover the salmon with further dill, and lay on it a board which will just fit into the top of the dish. Lay heavy weights on the board, and put the dish in a cool larder for 12 hours (or, in summer, it can be placed at the bottom of the refrigerator).

Blend all the ingredients for the sauce together and put in a bowl.

To serve the salmon, remove it from the dish. Put it on a board. Open it out and brush off the excess dill and pickling mixture. Cut fine slices on the bias. Serve with the sauce and brown bread and butter as accompaniments.

9
SALADS

Most firm cooked fish, when cold, make excellent salads, and shellfish are especially suitable. This sort of casual though satisfying dish can be dressed either richly with a mayonnaise (p. 21) or one of its variations, such as tartare sauce (p. 32) or gribiche (p. 31), or very simply with a plain vinaigrette (p. 21).

Of the firm fish, salmon, turbot, tuna, sea bass, bream and monkfish all make good Côte d'Azur-type salads, usually called nicoise, but which greatly vary in composition. Canned salmon and tuna are, I think, at their best when served and eaten in this way. This recipe can be adapted to take account of the ingredients available.

SALADE NICOISE

SERVES 4

1 lb/500 g of any of the fish named opposite, cut into small pieces

Other ingredients

4 oz/125 g French beans, diced

4 small potatoes, diced

4 tomatoes, peeled and sliced

2 hard-boiled eggs, roughly chopped

8 small fillets of anchovy

For garnish

8 black olives

2 teaspoons each of finely chopped tarragon, basil and chervil

Put the diced beans and potatoes in the middle of the salad dish and arrange the sliced tomatoes around the edge. Scatter the chopped eggs in the space between these two elements in the dish, and cover them with the pieces of fish. Lay the anchovies on top of the fish, so as to encircle the mound in the middle. Place the black olives, too, at intervals on top of the fish. Scatter the herbs over all, and sprinkle with a vinaigrette (p. 21).

Both fish and vegetables may be varied, substituting cooked diced celeriac or cooked diced fennel bulb for the French beans, for example, but if the salad is to retain its character it should always contain the tomatoes, the anchovies and the olives. As to the layout of the different elements in the dish to make the best effect, everyone will have a personal idea of arrangement and decor.

A SEAFOOD SALAD

SERVES 6

6 cooked scallops	2 cucumbers, peeled and sliced lengthwise into 4 in/10 cm sticks
1 lb/500 g cooked and flaked fish (such as fresh haddock or whiting)	
	¼ pt/150 ml aioli (p. 86)
1 tablespoon finely chopped parsley	6 medium tomatoes, peeled and halved horizontally
1 sweet red pepper, finely chopped	
	12 pitted black olives
5 hard-boiled eggs, very finely chopped	12 small cooked new potatoes, halved
¾ pt/450 ml taramasalata (p. 86)	a bunch of watercress
	12 small radishes
12 small cooked artichoke bottoms	12 lemon quarters
	1 large bowl of natural yogurt
1 large cos lettuce	

Dice the scallops into small cubes. Mix with the flaked fish, lightly, in a bowl, together with the parsley and the sweet red pepper.

Mix the hard-boiled eggs thoroughly with the taramasalata. Fill the artichoke bottoms with this mixture, which should be thick enough to be heaped up in mounds.

Cut the lettuce in fine strips and fluff it up into a chiffonade.

Select a large circular dish, and arrange the elements on it as follows. With the cucumber sticks make a reserve in the centre of the dish, into which ladle the diced scallops and flaked fish. Spoon the aioli carefully onto this fish mixture. Surround this reserve with the halved tomatoes, with an olive pressed into the centre of each. Now place the filled artichoke bottoms around the ring of tomatoes. Surround these concentric circles with the shredded lettuce on which distribute the potato halves. Fill the interstices of this display with small sprigs of watercress, radishes and quarters of lemon. Serve with a bowl of yogurt and with hot French bread and a strong red wine.

VARIATIONS

This is an obviously expandable recipe which, with the addition of other seafood, sauces and dips, can soon become a considerable buffet, or indeed a banquet. Consider the possibilities offered by half small lobsters, sliced, brushed with tartare sauce (p. 32) and laid, in the half shells, among the lettuce. Prawns, crawfish, dressed crabs, mussels, purées of vegetables, such as carrots, Jerusalem artichokes, mushrooms, etc. can all have their place. The only limitation is the cook's budget.

MIXED FISH SALAD

SERVES 4

3 scallops, poached and diced

4 large cooked prawns, peeled and cut in half, lengthwise

1 lb/500 g of any firm cooked fish, such as monkfish, sea bass or bream, cut in small pieces

1 large bunch of watercress

1 large carrot, cooked and shredded

1 tablespoon finely chopped parsley

For the vinaigrette

½ clove garlic, crushed

1 teaspoon sugar

½ teaspoon salt

1 teaspoon of made English mustard

1 tablespoon chopped shallots

1 tablespoon chopped chives

3 tablespoons wine vinegar

¼ pt/150 ml olive oil

Scatter the watercress over the salad dish. Mix all the pieces of fish and shellfish together in a bowl, and distribute them over the watercress. Sprinkle with the shredded carrot, then the parsley.

For the vinaigrette, pound all the ingredients, except the oil, with the vinegar. Now pour in the olive oil, and beat well together to amalgamate. Distribute the dressing carefully over the salad so that all the fish is anointed.

In the above recipe, both the fish and the vinaigrette are variable.

RATATOUILLE AND FISH SALAD

The Provençal ragoût, the ratatouille (p. 39), may be dressed with vinaigrette and served cold. It then makes an excellent salad with which cold shellfish or other firm fish can be served.

10
SOUPS

VELOUTE OF BRILL

Fish soups based on velouté and béchamel sauce should be a priority in the home kitchen. These soups are velvet-smooth, rich and nutritious, and make complete meals in themselves. This recipe can be made with all non-oily fish.

SERVES 4

8 oz/250 g of fillet of brill	2 egg yolks
1½ pt/900 ml of fish stock (p. 30)	2 oz/50 g butter
1 pt/600 ml fish velouté sauce (p. 20)	1 tablespoon white wine
	salt and pepper
¼ pt/150 ml single cream	**For garnish**
	watercress butter (p. 18)

Poach the fish in the stock for 3-4 minutes. Remove and pound it to a purée, then set aside. Strain the stock, and add the velouté sauce to it. Raise heat, and allow to simmer while stirring for 5-6 minutes. Remove from heat and stir in the purée of fish. Pass through a fine sieve. Return to the pan, and bring to simmering point. After a few minutes, remove from the heat, and allow to cool a little. Add the egg yolks, thoroughly beaten with the cream and a few tablespoons of the hot liquid. Stir all well together. Now work in the butter in small pieces. Heat the soup up to simmering point again, and allow to simmer very gently for a few minutes only. Add the wine, and taste for seasoning with salt and pepper.

VELOUTE OF MUSSELS

This is a velouté soup of the first distinction. Follow the previous recipe, but substitute for the fish stock 1½ pt/900 ml of the liquid in which mussels have been cooked (see moules marinière p. 62). Add this to the velouté sauce which, for this particular occasion, has been made with a fish stock strongly flavoured with leeks. Complete the process of thickening with egg yolks, cream and butter. Serve four or five poached mussels as garnish to each plate of soup. A grander version of this soup can be made by adding a purée of mussels themselves to the velouté. Serve with a parsley or fennel butter (p. 18).

FISH AVGOLEMONO SOUP

This soup is a simple, delicious and nourishing variant on a classic Greek dish.

SERVES 6-7

1 lb/500 g fillets of whiting, cod, hake, haddock or coley	1 tablespoon medium-dry white wine
3½ pt/2 litres rich fish stock (p. 30)	juice of 2 lemons
	pepper and salt, to taste
6 tablespoons long grain rice	2 tablespoons finely chopped parsley
	2 eggs

Poach the whiting in the stock for 6 or 7 minutes. Remove from the stock to a dish, and cut into small (½ oz/15 g) pieces. Set aside to cool. Now put the rice into the stock and cook quickly until tender. Remove from the heat to cool down. Meanwhile beat the eggs, wine and lemon juice together. Add to this a ladleful of the stock, and beat well. Incorporate this mixture into the body of the stock. Add the pieces of whiting. Season with pepper and salt. Replace the soup on the fire, and make piping hot but without allowing it to boil. At the last moment, just before serving, shower in the parsley. Ladle into very hot soup bowls and serve at once.

Note: the rich fish stock for this soup should include in its making a small red mullet and some small portions of cuttlefish, octopus or squid. The final excellence of the soup greatly depends on this enrichment of the stock.

CRAB AND LEEK SOUP

One of my favourite béchamel-based soups, this recipe can be made with other non-oily fish and shellfish.

SERVES 4

1 medium-sized freshly cooked crab	salt
	1¼ pt/750 ml water
the white of 4 leeks, finely chopped	1½ pt/900 ml béchamel sauce (p. 19)
4 or 5 sprigs and stalks of parsley	2 oz/50 g parsley butter (p. 18)
¼ pt/150 ml white wine	2 teaspoons chopped chives
a pinch of black pepper	
a pinch of cayenne pepper	lemon quarters

Break open and extract all the white and brown meat from the crab. Keep them separate and set aside.

Make a vegetable stock with the leeks, parsley, wine, pepper, salt and water. Boil this until it has reduced to 1 pt/600 ml. Mash the brown crab meat with a wooden spoon until smooth, and amalgamate it with the béchamel over low heat.

Loosen the mixture with the strained prepared stock, and simmer gently for 5 minutes. Season to taste, and fold in all the flaked white crab meat.

Ladle the soup into hot soup bowls. Add a pat of parsley butter and a sprinkle of chives to each bowl.

Serve with lemon quarters and brown bread and butter.

SHRIMP BISQUE

The bisque is an excellent soup based on a foundation of small quantities of rice cooked to a smooth paste.

SERVES 4

½ pt/300 ml water	pinch of saffron
½ pt/300 ml milk	1½ pt/900 ml single cream
1 lb/500 g fresh shrimps	
1 tablespoon pudding rice	1 tablespoon finely chopped parsley
1 bay leaf	
½ pt/300 ml white wine	salt and pepper to season

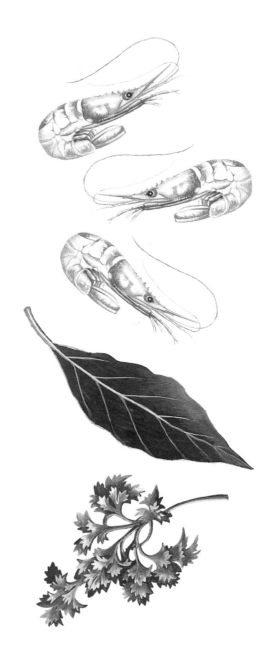

Put the mixture of milk and water into a saucepan and bring briskly to the boil. Wash the shrimps thoroughly. Throw them in, and cook for 2 minutes. Lift them out with a perforated slice, and put them aside on a plate to cool.

Strain the milk and water mixture into another pan. Add the rice and bay leaf, and allow to cook steadily as you shell the shrimps, leaving 4-5 of the larger ones unshelled. After cooking for half an hour, the rice will have begun to break up and the liquid to thicken. Put the peeled shrimps into a blender with 6 tablespoons of the liquid, and reduce to a thick purée. Return the purée to the pan. Add the wine, bring to simmering point, and cook for 6-7 minutes.

Infuse the saffron in a tablespoon of the hot liquid, and stir this into the soup. At this penultimate stage, chop up the unpeeled shrimps and blend them with their shells, into a purée, with half the cream. Pass this through a fine conical sieve into the soup. Now stir in the rest of the cream and the finely chopped parsley.

Note: a teaspoon of rouille or aioli (p. 86) provides a startling contrast in flavour which is exciting with this kind of soup. Prawns, scampi and crab also make fine rice-based bisques.

HAMPSTEAD HOTPOT

To make this fish stew, a fish kettle or an asparagus kettle with a draining tray is the best pan to use. If you don't have one, the tray of a pressure cooker and a large saucepan could be used instead.

SERVES 6

¼ pt/150 ml olive oil	6 oz/220 g squid
4 shallots, roughly chopped	8 oz/250 g monkfish tail fillet
2 cloves garlic	2 small red mullet
1 lb/500 g tomatoes	8 uncooked prawns
3 pt/1.8 litres boiling water	pinch of saffron or turmeric powder
¼ pt/150 ml white wine	salt, red and black pepper to season
7 oz/225 g whiting or dab	

Remove the draining tray from the kettle at the start of the operation. Heat the oil in the bottom of the kettle. Add the chopped shallots and garlic and cook until they are soft. Add the tomatoes, skinned and chopped, and continue to cook, mashing with a wooden spoon, until they have combined with the oil to form a purée. Pour in the boiling water and the white wine, and add the dab or whiting, and the squid, all cut in small pieces. Cook steadily for 20 minutes.

Now replace the draining tray in the kettle with the monkfish laid on it, and poach for 10 minutes. Add the red mullet and prawns, and cook gently for a further 8 minutes. Remove the kettle from the heat, and let it stand for 2 minutes. Lift the tray and transfer the monkfish, mullet and prawns to a hot dish. Replace the kettle on the heat, and boil briskly. Add the saffron, salt and pepper, and cook until the dab or whiting has disintegrated.

Meanwhile, cut the monkfish in small pieces, fillet the mullet, and shell the prawns. Immerse them on the tray in the kettle, not to cook further but simply to heat. Remove the tray once more. Put the fish in a deep hot dish. Ladle the boiling soup into hot bowls through a wide-meshed conical strainer, and add 2 teaspoons of aioli (p. 86) to each bowl. Serve with thick slices of toasted French bread.

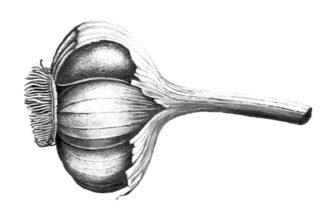

WATERZOOI

Waterzooi is a Belgian dish, usually made with fresh-water fish – perch is particularly good – but firm-fleshed sea fish such as monkfish, angel shark, turbot all make excellent waterzooi, as does the brill I have chosen here.

SERVES 4

2 lb/1 kg brill	2 sprigs thyme
4 shallots, finely chopped	1 bay leaf
1 carrot	salt and pepper
1 leek	pinch ground nutmeg
3 stalks celery	juice of ½ lemon
2 oz/50 g butter	4 tablespoons double cream (optional)
¼ pt/150 ml dry white wine	
¾ pt/450 ml rich fish stock (p. 30)	

Clean the carrot, leek and celery and cut them into thin julienne strips. Melt the butter in a large pan, put in the shallots and other vegetables and cook gently until they are soft. Do not let them brown.

Cut the brill into pieces weighing about 2 oz/ 50 g and put them on top of the vegetables. Pour the wine and stock over the fish, put in the thyme and bay leaf and season with salt, pepper and nutmeg.

Bring the contents of the pan to the boil, then lower the heat as far as possible, cover the pan and simmer gently for 10 minutes. There should be barely a bubble on the surface of the liquid.

Remove the fish to a warm tureen and keep warm. Stir the lemon juice into the cooking liquid and remove the thyme and bay leaf. Heat through, and if you are using cream stir it in now. Pour the stock over the fish and serve the stew in soup plates. Plain boiled potatoes go well with it.

DUTCH MUSSEL SOUP

SERVES 4-5

2 lb/1 kg small mussels	2 oz/50 g butter
½ bottle white wine	1¾ pt/1 litre water
1 large onion, chopped	salt and pepper
2 leeks, sliced	1 stalk celery, chopped very finely
1 carrot, diced	
1 thick slice celeriac, diced	

Clean the mussels thoroughly (see p. 61), and discard any that will not close (or feel too heavy). Put them in a large pan with the wine, cover and steam for a few minutes until the mussels open. Shake the pan from time to time. Remove the mussels from the pan and when they are cool enough to handle take them out of their shells and set aside. Discard any mussels that do not open. Pour any liquid from them back into the pan and strain all the cooking liquid through a muslin-lined sieve.

Melt the butter in a large heavy-bottomed pan and cook the onion, leeks, carrot and celeriac gently for 15 minutes. Do not let them brown. Add the water, the mussel liquid, a little salt and pepper and simmer for 20 minutes.

Add the finely chopped celery and simmer for a further 5 minutes. Return the mussels to the soup, heat through and serve hot.

—11—
MISCELLANEOUS FISH DISHES

In this chapter I have gathered a wide range of dishes – terrines, pâtés and mousses, pies and pilafs, quenelles, fish cakes and soufflés. In each case I have given one or two recipes to serve as patterns. They can be varied according to the fish available.

TERRINES

Fish terrines are simple dishes to make and can be much varied in flavour and texture. Basically they should combine a stiff purée of supporting fish, such as whiting, plaice or lemon sole, enriched by shellfish for flavour, with small whole fillets of a fine firm fish, such as Dover sole, brill, John Dory, turbot or halibut, to give body. These fillets are distributed evenly throughout the mixture, and the whole pressed down into a terrine, covered and cooked slowly in the oven in a bain-marie. The only liaison required for the purée is a minimum of egg, butter and double cream. Terrines may also combine a purée of fish and a purée of green vegetables to give a contrast of colour and taste. Whole fillets of fish may be used to line the dish and wrap around the forcemeat. They may be served cold, but not chilled, with a mayonnaise based sauce (see p. 58) or hot.

TERRINE OF DOVER SOLE WITH PRAWNS

SERVES 6

1 lb/500 g fillets of whiting, lemon sole or plaice

4 oz/125 g cooked and peeled prawns

4 large scallops, cleaned

1 large egg

4 fl oz/125 ml double cream

1 teaspoon turmeric powder

½ teaspoon salt

pinch of cayenne pepper

2 oz/50 g butter

1 lb/500 g fillets of Dover sole, cut into roughly 1 oz/25 g pieces

Pass the whiting, prawns, scallops and seasoning through a blender. Put the mixture into a bowl, and with a wooden spoon fold in the egg and cream, previously lightly beaten together. Season with turmeric, salt and cayenne and work the butter well in.

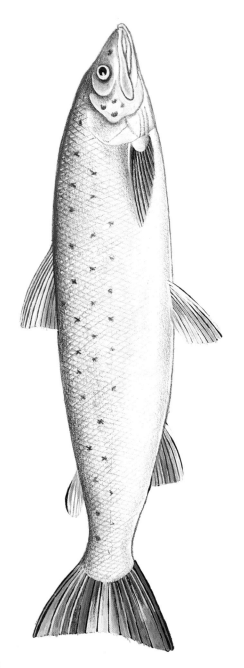

Put a layer of this mixture into the bottom of a 2 pt/1.2 litre terrine or soufflé dish, and scatter a few pieces of the Dover sole over it. Add more of the mixture, and again more pieces of the sole. Repeat until all ingredients have been used, finishing with a layer of purée. Cover. Cook in a bain-marie in the middle of a preheated oven (gas 3/325°F/160°C) for 2 hours. Serve with hollandaise sauce (p. 20), new potatoes and peas.

SALMON MOUSSE

Here is a sound basic recipe for a fish mousse, using fresh or canned salmon. However it can also be applied to most cooked fresh fish and to smoked fish. This is Anne Cavendish's recipe.

SERVES 6 as a first course

8 oz/250 g skinned, filleted, cooked salmon or two 6 oz/175 g cans of salmon, drained, skinned and boned

1 tablespoon tomato purée

1/4 pt/150 ml béchamel sauce (p. 19)

a good pinch of ground allspice

salt and pepper to season

1/2 oz/15 g gelatine

1/4 pt/150 ml any canned consommé that jells when cold

1/4 pt/150 ml whipped cream

2 whites of egg, stiffly beaten

Flake and pound the salmon with the tomato purée till smooth. Add the béchamel and the seasonings. Now dissolve the gelatine in the warmed consommé. Allow to cool, and mix thoroughly together with the fish mixture. As this begins to thicken, fold in the whipped cream and the stiffly beaten egg whites. Pour at once into a fish-shaped mould which has been very lightly brushed with olive oil. Chill in the refrigerator for at least 3 hours. Turn out onto a serving dish and garnish.

HERRING PATE

This recipe works well with all types of white fish, with salmon trout and the crustacea. For smoked fish, omit the anchovy fillets and use less salt.

SERVES 4-6

8 oz/250 g skinned, filleted, lightly cooked fresh herring

4 oz/125 g butter

1 shallot, finely chopped and pounded

1 tablespoon finely chopped parsley

3 anchovy fillets, pounded

½ clove garlic, crushed

pinch of cayenne pepper

1 teaspoon freshly ground black pepper

2 teaspoons Worcestershire sauce or any chosen relish (p. 16)

4 tablespoons fish fumet (p. 30) or of canned consommé

Blend all the ingredients except the fish fumet/consommé together into a smooth paste. Stir in the fumet, which should be cold and on the point of setting. Press the pâté firmly down into a terrine. Cover and put in the refrigerator to set. Serve very cold. If it is to be kept for more than 12 hours, seal it with a layer of melted butter before covering.

PATE STENDHAL

A handsome and simple pâté made with black and red lumpfish-roe 'caviar'; this is Suzanne O'Keeffe's recipe.

SERVES 12 as a first course

2½ oz/65 g jar black lumpfish roe

2½ oz/65 g jar red lumpfish roe

two 200 g packets creamery cheese

2 shallots very finely chopped

Blend the cheese with two very finely chopped shallots. Divide into two equal portions. Blend the red roe into one, and the black roe into the other. Arrange in an attractive round glass dish or terrine: half black and half red, or in alternating quarters. Chill for at least 3 hours and serve with Melba toast.

DIPS

The three recipes that follow can be served as dips with sticks of raw vegetables, biscuits or strips or pitta bread. They may be used as dressings for salads, to enrich soups or to serve as sauces with plainly cooked fish. They are indispensible to the fish cook.

ROUILLE

3 large cloves of garlic

2 large red peppers

2 anchovy fillets
the crumbs of one small white loaf (about 3 oz/75 g), soaked in milk and squeezed dry

3 tablespoons olive oil

¼ pt/150 ml good fish stock (p. 30)

1 teaspoon ground black pepper

Chop and pound the garlic, peppers and anchovies to a paste. Add the bread crumbs.

Work in the olive oil, and add the fish stock. Season with the freshly ground pepper. The rouille should not be too firm.

The above Mediterranean dip can also galvanize a fish soup or sauce.

AIOLI

Make a mayonnaise sauce (p. 21), and incorporate into it 6 cloves of garlic, crushed and pounded into a paste, with a little olive oil.

TARAMASALATA

This is the present-day successor, made with smoked cod's roe, to the original one made with the now almost unobtainable avgotarake (roe of a kind of grey mullet).

8 oz/250 g smoked cod's roe

2 cloves garlic, crushed and pounded

4 oz/125 g cream cheese

1 tablespoon freshly ground black pepper

1½ tablespoons olive oil

1 tablespoon lemon juice

Mix the cod's roe, garlic and cream cheese together thoroughly, seasoning with black pepper. Gradually work in first the olive oil, then the lemon juice.

SUBRICS OF FISH

These savoury morsels, based on a liberal use of egg yolk, make delectable hors d'oeuvres, or garnishes for other fish dishes, but can, on their own, provide a number of exciting dishes. The simplicity of their making is deceptive, and they are as useful as the coquille and cocotte gratins in the using up of surplus quantities of fish from previous operations. They can be looked on as miniature croquettes or crisp omelettes. They need not however be confined to leftovers. Should you have only 4 fillets of plaice in the house and 4 or more friends arrive, subrics will help to perform the miracle of feeding them.

FISH QUENELLES

These are small savoury dumplings made with a forcemeat of minced fish, seasonings and herbs, combined with a panada of light dough and egg, and then poached in salted water for 8-10 minutes. They are then drained, arranged decoratively on a serving dish, and dressed in a selected sauce. As almost every kind of fish, singly or mixed, can be used in them, and the seasonings and sauces can be widely varied, these dumplings offer another stimulus to invention in the kitchen. They also make extra garnishes to enhance and 'stretch' other fish dishes.

SUBRICS OF PLAICE

SERVES 6

1 lb/500 g fillets of poached plaice	6 oz/175 g mushrooms
8 oz/250 g potato, mashed without butter, milk or cream	1 teaspoon salt
	1 teaspoon black pepper
	1 pinch of ground nutmeg
6 egg yolks	3 oz/75 g clarified butter (unsalted will do)
1 shallot, finely chopped	

Cut up the fillets of plaice, and mix them into the potato, mashing them well, to form a homogenous thick mixture. Beat in the 6 egg yolks, the shallots and the seasonings. You will now have a loose mixture of the consistency of very thick cream. In a frying pan, heat the butter until very hot. Using a tablespoon, drop the mixture, spoonful by spoonful, into the piping hot butter. The underside of each subric will crisp very quickly, and a fringe of egg will seep around it. Flip over, and cook till seepage of the egg on the second side ceases. Whip out quickly with a draining spoon and arrange on a heated serving dish. The above quantities should provide up to 30 subrics. Serve with carrots, cooked and then caramelized, and courgettes or green beans.

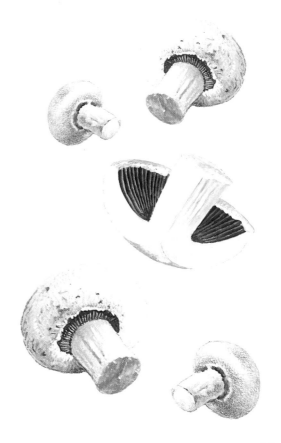

CRAB AND WHITING QUENELLES

SERVES 6-8

For the forcemeat

8 oz/250 g whiting fillets

12 oz/375 g cooked crabmeat, ¾ white, ¼ brown

2 pounded anchovy fillets

1 clove garlic, finely chopped

1 shallot finely chopped

1 tablespoon finely chopped parsley

1 tablespoon finely chopped thyme

½ teaspoon cayenne pepper

2 eggs

juice of ½ lemon

For the panada

5 oz/150 g plain flour

4 egg yolks

4 oz/125 g melted butter

generous pinch ground nutmeg

generous pinch ground allspice

7 fl oz/200 ml boiling milk

Make the panada first as, when made, it should be allowed to get quite cold and then stand in the refrigerator for at least 30 minutes before using. With a wooden spoon, blend the flour with the egg yolks. Pour in the butter. Add the seasonings and stir vigorously. Then pour in the boiling milk very slowly, as you work the mixture well with the spoon. Remove to a pan, and on a low heat, cook very gently for 6 minutes, at the same time beating with a whisk. Spread the mixture out on a flat, buttered dish. Cover with buttered paper, and when cold put in the refrigerator for 30 minutes.

For the forcemeat, blend all the ingredients together into a stiff paste. Combine both panada and forcemeat together, and blend by thoroughly kneading by hand in a large bowl, or use a food processor.

Have a wide pan full of simmering salted water on the stove, and then scoop out rounded tablespoons of the mixture, and, keeping the shape of the spoon, lower them gently into the water, which should completely cover them. Let them simmer for 6 minutes.

It is best to cook these quenelles in batches of, say, 6 at a time, so that the temperature of the water and the timing can be easily controlled. Remove the quenelles with a draining spoon and arrange them in a heated dish. Serve with a rich tomato sauce (p. 35) or a sweet and sour sauce (p. 41).

FISH SOUFFLE

Although many people are intimidated by imaginary difficulties in making a soufflé, this is a simple dish, though one we tend to order in a restaurant rather than make at home. This recipe applies to all varieties of cooked or smoked fish.

SERVES 2-3

8 oz/250 g cooked fish

¼ pt/150 ml thick béchamel sauce (p. 19)

3 egg yolks

4 egg whites

Preheat the oven to gas 4/350°F/180°C. Put a baking tin on the middle shelf to get hot. Pound the fish to a smooth purée, and amalgamate it with the béchamel (this can be done in a food processor). Beat the egg yolks well in. Warm and butter the inside of a 7 in/18 cm soufflé dish. Now beat the egg whites to a stiff froth, and fold them lightly and quickly into the mixture. Pour the mixture out of the mixing bowl into the soufflé dish as quickly as you can. Shake level. Put the dish on the hot baking tin. Cook for 25 minutes. Serve immediately.

FISH PIES

Fish pie should be a regular once-a-week dish in the home. As the contents can be so easily varied, it never becomes monotonous. Permute three of its elements each week: the kind of fish; the herbs and seasonings; and the pie covering. One constant remains, and that is a fish velouté sauce.

SIMPLE FISH PIE

This recipe can serve as a pattern for the construction of fish pies.

SERVES 4-6

½ lb/250 g cod	1 pt/600 ml thickish
½ lb/250 g hake	velouté sauce (p. 20)
5 oz/150 g sole fillets	**For covering**
1 large or 2 small scallops	1½ lb/750 g well-
court-bouillon (p. 28)	buttered but stiffish
3 hard-boiled eggs, coarsely chopped	mashed potato
2 teaspoons finely chopped parsley and capers	

Poach the fish in the court-bouillon for 3-5 minutes, depending on whether they are soft or firm. Remove to a plate. Skin and fillet where necessary, and chop up, but not too finely.

Lay the fish in a pie dish with the chopped eggs. Sprinkle with the parsley and capers. Pour the velouté sauce over all, and shake the dish well so that the sauce fills all the spaces under and between the ingredients. Cover with the mashed potato. Pattern the top with a fork, and put in the oven at gas 5/375°F/190°C for 20 minutes or till the top is well browned.

VARIATIONS

Introduce as a shellfish element a few poached mussels, chopped cooked prawns or whole shrimps, white crab meat or cockles. Vary the main fish at your inclination and according to the state of your budget.

To vary the seasonings for the pie, enrich the potato with finely chopped fennel and 2 teaspoons finely chopped chives; or work into the potato 4 oz/125 g of very dry cooked spinach, and sprinkle with Parmesan cheese. As an alternative covering, use puff or shortcrust pastry.

SALMON FISH CAKES

For fish cakes made with cooked or canned fish, this is a simple general recipe, bearing in mind that herbs and seasonings can be varied at will.

SERVES 5-6

one 7 oz/200 g can salmon	1 lb/500 g mashed potato, without milk or cream
1 tablespoon finely chopped parsley	3 egg yolks, lightly beaten
1 tablespoon finely chopped chives	2 oz/50 g fine breadcrumbs
1 teaspoon horseradish cream	oil or butter for shallow frying
1 teaspoon anchovy essence	

Thoroughly drain the salmon. Put it into a large mixing bowl, and pound it, bones and all, into a paste.

Add the parsley, chives, horseradish cream and anchovy essence, and amalgamate with the salmon. Next add the mashed potato, a little at a time, until you have a homogenous thick mixture.

With the hands, knead the mixture into small 2 oz/50 g cylinders. Roll them in the beaten egg yolks, then in the fine breadcrumbs. Let them stand, covered, for 1 hour before cooking.

Shallow fry the fish cakes in oil or clarified butter, frequently shaking the pan and rolling the cakes around until nicely browned all over. Drain, and serve on a hot dish, surrounded by grilled tomato halves, each topped with a generous pat of a savoury butter (p. 18).

FISH PILAFS

These are economical fish dishes, unless of course we insist on using lobster, crawfish, crayfish, scallops or scampi. However, mussels and prawns should be within the reach of most of us.

Here is a pattern recipe for all fresh fish. If fish canned in oil are substituted, they must be drained and rinsed in warm water before using.

TUNA PILAF

SERVES 8

1 lb/500 g poached fresh tuna	2 shallots, finely chopped
4 oz/125 g unsalted butter	1 tablespoon finely chopped capers
1 large red pepper, deseeded and finely chopped	3 small fillets of anchovy, chopped
1 large green pepper, deseeded and finely chopped	3 hard-boiled eggs, grated
	7 oz/200 g long-grain rice

Flake the tuna, and set aside to keep hot. In a frying pan put 2 oz/50 g of butter, and lightly sauté the peppers and the shallots. Gently mix in the flaked tuna, the capers, anchovies and eggs. Set aside and keep hot.

Boil the rice for 12½ minutes. Drain well, and dry out under a cloth in the bottom of a very low oven. Each grain should be separate. Now put the rice into a large hot bowl or dish, and quickly spoon onto it the fish and other ingredients. Using two large forks, lift the rice up from the bottom, so that the ingredients are spread evenly throughout it. Dot the dish with small pieces of the remaining butter. Cover and put into a moderate oven (gas 4/350°F/180°C) for 10 minutes, to heat through.

Serve with an aioli (p. 86) or a rouille (p. 86) and a good red wine.

KEDGEREE

Immortal kedgeree! Here, it is made with smoked haddock.

SERVES 8

2 lb/1 kg smoked haddock, filleted and flaked	3 hard-boiled eggs, roughly chopped
7 oz/200 g long-grain rice, cooked as in preceding recipe for tuna pilaf	1 tablespoon finely chopped parsley
5 oz/150 g butter	1 tablespoon finely ground black pepper

Into a piping hot deep dish, put the cooked rice and the butter, lightly using a wide-pronged fork to distribute the latter throughout. Now put in all the other ingredients, and again use a wide-pronged fork to distribute them evenly throughout the rice. Cover and put into a preheated low oven, gas 2/300°F/150°C for 10 minutes, to get really hot.

There it is in all its simplicity. Smoked cod and whiting can be substituted for haddock, but it is not quite the same.

SEAFOOD AURORE

This is a sound and variable recipe. It provides a good basis for a seafood pilaf.

SERVES 4

8 large prawns, peeled

4 scallops, cleaned

24 mussels, cleaned

1 finely chopped shallot

4 parsley stalks

2 sprigs fennel

1 pt/600 ml white wine

1 pt/600 ml water

salt and black pepper to season

6 oz/175 g long-grain rice, cooked

For the sauce aurore

½ pt/300 ml soubise sauce (p. 31)

2 tablespoons tomato purée

1 tablespoon chopped basil

Put the shallot, parsley, fennel and seasonings into the wine and water, and bring to the boil. Now put in the prawns, and boil for 3 minutes. Then add the scallops to simmer for a further 5 minutes. With a draining spoon remove the prawns and scallops to a covered dish, and set aside.

Put in the mussels, cover, and boil briskly for a minute or two, shaking the pan, until all the mussels are open.

Remove the mussels to drain in a colander on a dish to catch any juices still coming from them. Add these juices to the liquid in the pan, and boil quickly to reduce the liquid by half. Add this residue to the aurore sauce, which is made by adding tomato purée and basil to soubise sauce.

Arrange the rice around the edge of a deep serving dish. Place the seafood in the centre and pour the sauce over them.

Garnish the rice with thick pats of a savoury butter (p. 18), and sprinkle with freshly ground black pepper.

INDEX